Wishing Well

A Guide to Creating Your Dreams Through Cosmic Ordering

Steven Hall MCOH MASC NLP

Special Thanks to

Natalie, Robin, John
Owen, Sarah, Mum and Dad

The author of this book does not dispense medical advice or recommend the use of any technique in this book for the treatment of psychological or physical conditions without the advice of a qualified professional. This information is provided with the intent of improving your life and developing your spiritual well being. The author and publisher of this work can assume no responsibility for your actions or the results you achieve by following the advice and suggestions herein.

Contents

Introduction

In the beginning, this book didn't start here; it started at chapter 2. Chapter 1, about to follow, didn't exist. As I was writing about the techniques, it suddenly dawned on me that I didn't have a quality example that could show you the techniques in action. Don't get me wrong, I'd used these techniques numerous times to create all sorts of things, but none of them had that 'wow factor' that I'd be looking for as a reader. So, I stopped writing mid-flow and got to thinking...

"What do I want that I can create right now, which will be a great example of cosmic ordering in action?"

The one thing that I wanted more than anything was to move to a new home! So, the original chapter 1 was shunted aside to later become chapter 2, and I began a real-time experiment that was to become the new start to the book. This was to be a demanding test. There were several obstacles that stood in the way of a new home. If it worked though, it'd be a great example of cosmic ordering in action. So, it was time to go....

House Hunting

My partner Natalie and I had been 'conventional' house hunting for almost three years then. We'd looked at hundreds of houses ranging from £100k to £250k but nothing managed to tick all the boxes. I'd resisted using cosmic ordering for something as big and expensive as a house because I felt it was simply too much to ask for, even though I'd been very successful with everything else I'd ordered so far. I was worried that if I used cosmic ordering on a house and it didn't appear, I might begin to doubt that it was real. I was so scared of failure that I couldn't even bring myself to try.

Our purely physical efforts had reaped no reward, and as I found myself searching for an example with the 'wow factor' to illustrate the awesome power of cosmic ordering in action, it seemed only logical that I should order a house. I sat myself down and began to create my new home wish list.

Knowing that the more detailed and specific I made my list, the greater the chances that I'd get what I was looking for, I grabbed a notepad and began scribbling down absolutely everything that I wanted from my new home. The list was extensive. I'm not going to reproduce it all here, but I have included the main points that we felt were most important.

- A large private garden with mature plants
- A large garage for sculpture work
- Space for a soundproof recording studio
- Three bedrooms
- Wooden floorboards
- Attractive wood frame windows
- Potential for improvement
- Close to my parents' home - and our friends
- Between £145k and £150k
- A large patio area for BBQ parties
- A quiet street (to keep our cat safe!)
- Located on the east side of town.

I also listed a few requirements that would need to be addressed before we would be able to get a mortgage. We had no deposit to put down and a hefty credit card debt to consider. I had no idea how, but I wanted those two situations sorted before even thinking about looking at mortgage options.

Once my list was complete, I went through the same cosmic ordering processes I'd used in the past to create smaller things and then stopped looking at houses and left everything in the hands of the cosmos. Over the following month, I not only forgot about the order I'd placed, but I also forgot that we were even looking for a new home. I began to really appreciate the flat and focused on my business.

Within a couple of months, something strange happened. Totally out of the blue, my aunt gave me £5,000. This unexpected windfall came with a reservation that got me thinking about house hunting again. My aunt hated seeing money go to waste, and having discovered that I'd been renting for almost 10 years, she thought she'd step in. As far as she was concerned, renting was dead money and she had a very good point. During my extended residence in a one bedroom flat, I had spent a total of £36,720 on rent alone!

Considering how much 'dead money' I'd wasted over the years, the stipulated reservation that came with this generous and unexpected gift was very fitting: the £5,000 had to be used as a deposit on a house. I was chuffed to bits! The first piece of my cosmic order was in the palm of my hand! I hadn't a clue where the money for the deposit was going to come from and would never have dreamed that a relative would simply give it to me.

Thursday, 12th July 2007

Armed with my £5,000 deposit fund, I logged on to the Internet and began hunting for my perfect home. I found a local estate agent's website and began browsing through the properties on offer. The site had its own search feature, so I selected three bedrooms, the town where I wanted to live, and a price range of £145k to £150k. The search returned twelve results that matched my criteria. Of those twelve, four looked worthy of further inspection. I immediately booked viewing appointments for those four, all of which were scheduled for the following day.

Friday, 13th July 2007

We went to look at the first two properties in the morning. Both had potential, but fell far short of our expectations. As we left the second property, my enthusiasm was waning. I'd been in this position many times before. Trying to find a home that was perfect was a tall order, especially when I'd concocted such an extensive list of requirements. I obviously didn't expect to tick every box on my list, but it would be nice to be able to tick the main ones.

The third and fourth viewing appointments were scheduled for later in the afternoon, so I went back to the flat and reviewed my list. Looking at the list a little more realistically, I began crossing off anything that wasn't absolutely essential and hi-lighting the points that we simply couldn't do without. I was less than halfway through the list when I decided that if I was going to manifest a new home with the power of cosmic ordering, then I should do it properly! If I wanted wooden floors throughout my home, I should get them! If I wanted mature plants in my garden, then I should have those too! I stopped crossing things off and hi-lighted every single point on the list. I then read them all out loud as though I already had them.

Part of me knew that the list was unrealistic. This part of me had already accepted that a house that perfectly matched my extensive criteria probably doesn't even exist anywhere, let alone on the east side of the small town where I'd ordered it to be. My cosmic order was beginning to feel more like a tall order. Another part of me thought very differently though, and that's the part of me that I chose to listen to.

This part of me knew that placing an order with the cosmos was very similar to calling up a friend on the telephone. If I wanted to talk to a particular friend, I'd have to dial the correct number. I needed every single digit or it simply wouldn't work. If I got the number wrong, mixed it up, or left some out, I wouldn't get to talk to my friend. I'd probably get to talk to someone, but it wouldn't be what I truly wanted. I might not even get to speak to anyone at all and would have totally wasted my time. Crossing out points on my list was like missing out numbers on the dial. I placed the order to receive a very specific home, and I wasn't about to change my order now that the delivery process had already begun. All I had to do was wait for it to arrive.

I trusted the cosmos and believed in the power of creation much more than I doubted that a house can tick all the boxes on my list, even if some of them were a little fastidious. We had about an hour or so to kill before leaving to view the third property, so I decided to do a clearing meditation to help ease the delivery of my cosmic order. During the meditation, I could clearly see myself in my dream home. It felt so close and tangible. I could feel a tremendous sense of acceptance, but not just from me. It was as though the house itself had ordered us to live there just as eagerly as I'd ordered it to live in. It felt like a cooperative process of companionship, like two long distance friends finally meeting. I enjoyed the experience for a few minutes then continued to perform a magnetising meditation to help speed things along.

Everything seemed to be going so well that I decided to add a few extra points to my list. I'd already ordered wooden floors throughout, but thought it'd be more practical to have quarry tiles as you entered the house (wet shoes and wooden floor boards probably wasn't a great idea). I'd also stated that I wanted mature plants in the garden, which got upgraded to a fruit tree.

I wanted to build a soundproof studio, but having done a little research on soundproofing a room, I'd discovered how difficult it was. Soundproofing a room with floorboards was almost impossible; the noise simply travels along the gap under the floor. To prevent this, I needed to put the studio on a solid floor, but I'd ordered wooden floors throughout! My original plan was to convert the spare bedroom, but it now seemed more logical to put it in the garage, so I needed a much bigger garage!

I made a few more new demands, such as friendly, quiet neighbours and an attractive road. The houses we'd viewed in the morning required driving through some very unsightly areas, and I think it's important to enjoy the scenery on your way home, so I extended my order to the surrounding area. Our new home had to be in an attractive part of town on a tree-lined road with lots of beautiful gardens. With my updated list and absolute faith in the power of the cosmos, we set out to view property number three.

This house wasn't vacant, so our viewing appointment had been arranged with the current owners. As we set off, I couldn't help thinking about all of the points on my list. So far, nothing had come close to ticking them all, although to be honest, some were rather trivial! Nevertheless, I was eager to find out how this house would do and left the flat with an almost nervous sense of excited anticipation.

I knew the area very well as the address was very close to where my father grew up, on the east side of town (TICK!). I'd spent many long Sunday afternoons watching Big Daddy and Giant Haystacks battle it out in the ring while Granddad snoozed in his chair and the smell of Gradma's freshly baked goodies wafted in from the kitchen.

The area had changed from how I remembered it; most notably the tall luscious trees that lined the entire road. (TICK!) I was also immediately struck by how quiet the street was. I recalled several cars driving past my grandparents' house as a child, but this road was towards the back of the estate with no through roads and no reason to drive down it unless you lived here… our cat would be perfectly safe! (TICK!)

Every garden we passed as we closed in on number 31 revealed the tremendous sense of pride that the people living on this street had. Each was a splendid feast of colour and texture: beautiful flowers, well groomed lawns, and creeping ivy hugging old brick walls in a warming embrace. Each home was bursting with character and personality. That was a road that I'd enjoy walking down for many years. (TICK!)

The 'For Sale' sign was now in clear view and, as we pulled up at the property, we both immediately commented on the windows. They were exactly how I'd imagined them, even though I'd seen nothing similar on any other property ever! As we were welcomed in, a few things immediately struck me. This property felt right. I was very sensitive to the energy of a building, and this one was tremendously welcoming. Stepping in through the doorway, I noticed the quarry tiles beneath my feet and smiled, acknowledging my updated list as I mentally ticked off another box.

We made our way into the living room, and I was stunned at what lay before us. We'd previously seen this room on the estate agent's website. From the image online, I remembered a hideous dark brown carpet and had already planned to lay laminate flooring throughout this area. But… this was no longer necessary. The awful carpet was simply a victim of poor photography. It was actually an incredibly beautiful rug, which was hiding an even more impressive real wood floor. Wooden floors on the ground floor of a property in this town were very unusual. As most properties were built following the blitz and had poured concrete floors, this was a pleasant and unexpected surprise. However, wooden floors were on my list, so we should have expected them!

As we made our way through the property, it became apparent that my order for wooden floors had been taken very seriously. Every room and even the stairs had original wooden floorboards, all beautifully smoothed and treated. The only areas that were not adorned with such splendour were those you'd step onto as you entered the property from the front or back doors. And both of these had quarry tile flooring, just as I'd ordered.

The property occupied a corner plot, so the garden was larger than expected. It was well stocked with plenty of mature plants and completely private. One side was an 8ft fence and the other a 10ft hedge. Stepping out from the back of the house led to a large paved patio area that would be perfect for social gatherings and midsummer night barbecues. This alone ticked all the requirements of my original list. But the most impressive feature was the 50-year-old apple tree that stood proudly in the centre of the lawn. Perfect!

From the garden, we made our way into the garage, which was huge! Much bigger than a conventional garage, easily capable of accommodating the soundproof studio, the sculpture workshop, and a large family car. I wanted to build the studio myself but knew that I'd need a qualified electrician to increase the number of power points. Not any more. The garage boasted six electrical sockets situated exactly where I'd be putting the studio. This was perfect and meant that I could build the studio all by myself without making a mess in the house!

It seemed strange that the property had such unusual features that fit my order so perfectly. It turned out that the previous owners had a mechanics business and built a larger than average garage to accommodate their specific needs. More unusual than this was the story behind the windows. The lady that was showing us around the property actually designed the windows herself and commissioned a French builder to make them. They were exactly as I'd imagined them to be. I didn't previously know if such windows even existed, but I knew what I wanted. Now I know that this three bedroom house with its perfect garden, wooden floors, and a larger than average garage situated along an attractive tree lined road on the east side of town is probably the only house in the entire world that has those exact windows!

As we continued our tour of the property, every single specification on my list was ticked. We immediately knew that this was going to be our new home; it even ticked boxes we weren't too bothered about! I'd stipulated that the property needed to be near to my friends', as well as my parents' address. It was almost exactly halfway between the two! It had tremendous potential for improvement by extending out on top of the existing garage to create two extra bedrooms and, being on the market for £149,950, was just inside our specified price range of £145k – £150k. We only went on to view the fourth property after this one as we had no way of cancelling the appointment and knew the occupant was waiting for us.

The following morning we put in an offer for £145k. It was declined. The estate agent informed us that another couple had also put in an offer on the property that had been declined. Although the seller refused both offers, they did specify a price they would accept. The estate agent told us that the other couple had first refusal on this price and would call us back to let us know their decision.

We waited by the phone.

That weekend was probably the longest weekend of my life. We were beginning to regret not offering the full asking price. The house was so perfect it would be such a shame to lose it now.

Monday, 16th July 2007

The estate agent finally called back. The other couple had decided not to stretch to the updated price, so we were next in line. All we had to do was say yes! The new asking price was £147,500, smack in the middle of my pre-ordered price window... to the penny! We immediately said 'YES!'

Although we'd now put in an offer that had been accepted, we still had only £5,000 towards a deposit and a hefty credit card balance to clear before we wanted to take on mortgage repayments. Ideally, we wanted to double the deposit to £10k and pay off our existing debts before moving. Excluding the £5,000 we already had, we were over £11,000 short, which we needed to find in less than two months. But we didn't have to wait those two months. Within two days, the £11,000 found us—£5k from Natalie's parents to help boost the deposit fund and the other £6k from mine to clear my credit card debt! Given that we'd now received £16,000 from family, you'd be forgiven if you thought this was a regular occurrence, or that forking out thousands of pounds 'willy-nilly' was something our relatives could easily afford to do. It wasn't. Without going into the details, each of these cash windfalls followed a bizarre yet synchronistic path to reach us, and every one was in perfect time and perfect order, just as is always the case when you surrender to the power of the cosmos.

Immediately after making the offer on the property, I handed in the required two months notice on the flat, giving us eight weeks to do whatever it was that you needed to do when you bought a new house. This was our first un-rented property, so we hadn't got a clue what the process was, but eight weeks seemed like it'd be more than adequate to have everything sorted.

Friday, 20th July 2007

A letter dropped through my door today to confirm receipt of the said two months notice. However, for some bizarre reason, our landlord seemed incapable of processing anything that wasn't based on a whole calendar month, so our eight-week deadline had now grown to almost ten. This meant that the last day of our current tenancy was now 30th September which, as fate would have it, was a Sunday. This would give us the whole weekend to move, which was very handy as the flat was situated inside a pedestrian zone and traffic restriction (enforced by rising bollards) prevented us from getting a removal truck within 100 yards of the flat during the week!

Now that we had a set date to be out of the flat, we needed a set date before it to be in the house! Because the flat tenancy expired on a Sunday and solicitors don't tend to work the weekend, our ideal date was the previous Friday (September 28th) or sometime before. The closer to the 28th we moved, the cheaper it would be. If we exchanged too early, we'd have to pay rent and mortgage payments for the overlapping period. If we exchanged too late, we'd need to pay storage costs, shift all of our stuff twice, and have to find somewhere temporary to live! So ideally, financially and practically, Friday, 28th September, was the perfect day to move. Logic and reason all pointed to the 28th, but it seemed such a long way off, and we were really eager to get out of the flat as soon as possible. The flat came with its fair share of problems, most annoying of which were the neighbours. They were well-meaning people, but incredibly noisy. They'd spend almost all day shouting to each other while standing on the fire escape (which was directly outside of our living room window!) This was more than a nuisance while watching TV, it made meditation practically impossible and totally ruled out the possibility of working with clients at the flat.

Shutting the window just muffled the noise, and I'd lost count of the number of times I'd politely asked them to try to keep it down. Even though I was usually very aware of my own resistance to situations, I hadn't really noticed how much I'd let this disturbance get to me. It usually began at around 8am and was pretty much constant until at least 7 or 8pm.

Particularly annoying were the mobile phone calls; these were always made outside on the fire escape and were very loud! Even with all the windows closed, we could clearly hear every single word and our neighbours spent a lot of time on the phone!

As soon as we found out that we were definitely moving, the noise didn't really seem to bother us any more. Knowing that we wouldn't have to put up with it much longer made it much more tolerable! There's a saying you'll come across a lot as you explore different ways to create your reality: 'Whatever you resist, persists!' It's not until you actually stop resisting something that you can move away from it. This was exactly what happened a week or so later when two of the noisiest neighbours suddenly moved out without notice on the same day!

Their unexpected move meant that the flat was now incredibly peaceful and actually a very pleasant place to live. This sudden change of circumstances meant that we were more than happy staying for those extra two weeks, and now everything pointed to Friday, 28 September, as the perfect time to move.

Over the next few weeks, there seemed to be a string of ridiculous events that were totally out of our control, all perfectly designed to slow down the process and drag everything out for twice as long as it should take. Our mortgage advisor left Natalie's passport in a photocopier, and the mortgage provider wouldn't release the funds until they got to see it. Our solicitor didn't seem to be able to get hold of my accountant to verify my employment status, and no one could get in contact with the vendor. For a long time, we could only assume that they were on holiday.

The problems actually began almost immediately. Only days after we had put in the offer, our file was assigned to someone that was about to take two weeks leave, and it sat on her desk, untouched, throughout that entire period! Fortunately for us, all of these delays meant that we definitely wouldn't be paying mortgage and rent payments that overlapped. But it did mean there was a very high possibility of our being homeless!

Throughout the entire situation both Natalie and I always felt completely secure and confident that we'd be moving on 28th September. The date was just so perfect that we couldn't see any way that it wouldn't happen. Friends, who were going through the same process, insisted that something would go wrong or the seller would pull out at the last minute. Neither our solicitor nor the vendor's estate agent could see us completing by this date, but we remained totally convinced that it would happen.

Thursday, 20th September 2007

Things finally seemed to be moving along, albeit very slowly! We finally met our solicitor to sign the papers. This left just eight days for everything else to fall into place. At this stage, we still didn't know if the mortgage company were prepared to release the funds. Our mortgage had already been changed twice; my self-employed status (without any accounts available) and Natalie's only working a three-day week already vastly limited our options. Our £10,000 deposit fell well short of the mandatory 10%, so as far as

17

mortgage offers were concerned, if this one fell through we didn't have an alternative. We still couldn't contact the vendors and for some bizarre reason our file had a post-it note attached to it stating that I was working away until 3rd October and nothing could proceed until I got back! Being a self employed writer and therapist, I work from home and create my own schedule, so I'd be available absolutely any time of any day that anyone needed me. The only conclusion that I could come to was that the post-it wasn't meant for our file, even though it did have mine and Natalie's full names on it!

Monday, 24th September 2007

We now had just 6 days before we vacated the flat and only four days before the final opportunity to complete and exchange contracts! I popped in to see the vendor's estate agent to ask if they could shed any light on what was going on. While I was in their office, they called the vendor but still couldn't get through. They contacted the vendor's solicitor, but they had no idea what was going on either. In fact, although they tried, they weren't really able to help much at all but took my mobile number and promised to call me back if they found anything out.

On my way home, I popped into a few department stores to hunt for new ornaments. The possibility of anything falling through was still completely alien to me. I was totally certain that it'd somehow be alright. I'd cosmically ordered everything to happen in perfect order with perfect timing, and Friday the 28th was still the perfect day to move. While in the department, store my phone rang. I'd only been out of the estate agent's about 15 minutes, but in those few short minutes, it seemed that everything had fallen into place. The estate agent had cleared up the 3rd October blunder and finally managed to contact the vendors and communicate with both solicitors to arrange for completion and exchange to take place that week. When I asked for a date, the woman on the other end of the phone told me that the keys to the house would be ready for collection from 9am on Friday the 28th of September... Perfect!

What is Cosmic Ordering?

Cosmic ordering is a method of attracting something into your reality through conscious manipulation of your focus, emotions, and beliefs. This means that by mastering cosmic ordering, you are actually able to create your own reality... consciously. Creating your own reality isn't new; you've been doing it all your life. The only difference now is that you're about to learn how to do it consciously. In a nutshell, the cosmic ordering process is simply choosing to have something, shifting your focus and belief about having it, magnetising it to you through the power of your emotions, and allowing it to manifest in your life. The entire process works because of universal spiritual laws that govern all things. It makes absolutely no difference who is placing the cosmic order—a sinner or a saint, a pauper or a tycoon. Cosmic ordering is an exact spiritual science, and as long as you follow the ordering process correctly, you cannot fail to manifest into your life whatever it is that you desire.

This book explores that process in detail giving you access to proven techniques specifically designed to make cosmic ordering easy. These techniques will help you stretch your beliefs on what is possible and cause you to think in new and exciting ways. Here, you'll discover some incredibly simple ways to begin living the life you desire, as well as many powerful techniques to enhance the entire process in ways that have never previously been revealed.

But before we get into all that, I want to explore an area that very few people have the privilege of enjoying. And that's...

Creating Your Desires Naturally

Not too many years ago, a close friend told me what he wanted out of life. His words painted a picture on the canvas of my imagination that revealed his ideal reality. His vision of the future wasn't too extraordinary, but it was a far cry from his current situation. He created images of a nice quiet family home, a pet dog, a beautiful wife, and a rewarding career. When we had that conversation, we were both working at the local pizza delivery shop. He was single, had no pets, and was sharing a house with three friends, all of whom were in a very similar situation. Back then, it didn't seem as though anything could ever change. The 'lads' had a set routine that merged all of the days into one. They rarely went out, so it was unlikely that he'd meet a girl, let alone marry one, and as days turned into weeks and weeks into months, his vision of the future looked as though it would never be anything more than a fantasy.

My friend didn't have a plan as such, but he did have an extremely clear vision of what he wanted.

Over the following couple of years, I watched as his vision of the future slowly became his reality. First came a significant change of career. He joined the police force, which he found incredibly rewarding. He continually strived to better himself within the force, regularly taking on additional duties and submitting himself to various training programs. His commitment and dedication to his career was recently rewarded as he passed his sergeants exam. While training as a police officer, the second part of his life plan started falling into place. He'd met and fallen in love with a fellow recruit, and although they lived almost the length of the country apart, they were both stationed at the same training ground and quickly became very good friends. By the time the training was complete, their friendship had blossomed into a loving relationship, and she moved in to the shared house.

A need for privacy soon allowed the third piece of the picture to begin forming, as they secured their place on the property ladder and bought a small house of their own. As their first property, it was a compromise on the vision, but it did enable the final piece to fall into place. This was a beautiful German Shepherd that had been removed from the police dog training program due to a fear of heights.

The relationship quickly took a step up the ladder of commitment as they tied the knot. Within a couple of years, they moved again—this time to a larger property in a quiet cul-de-sac exactly how my friend had described it to me as we stood in the office of the pizza shop only a few years ago. Now the family is expanding with their first baby born in February, and it is safe to say that the vision of the future my friend once shared with me has indeed become his reality.

You probably know someone yourself that has a similar story to tell, and we all know lots of people for whom nothing ever seems to happen. The difference between these two doesn't come down to luck or chance, and it's not about being in the right place at the right time, although this may often seem like the case. The difference is…

Focus

When you ask a group of people what they want out of life, only a tiny fraction will actually tell you. The rest think they're telling you, but they're not. What they do tell you is what they don't want out of life, and they do it incredibly well. The difference between focusing on what you want to achieve and focusing on what you don't is enormous. This is one of the most important steps in the conscious living process. If you want to create your own reality, a positive focus on the direction you want to travel is paramount to your success.

My friend is one of the lucky few that do this automatically. When he thinks of something he wants, he sees it in his mind's eye clearly. His thoughts actually create the substance that represents the object of his focus in a higher dimension to which we usually have no conscious access. Over time, his continued focus, like a magnet, draws this creation to him, and before long, it filters down into the physical world to become his reality. If you hold a clear image in your mind of what you want, sooner or later you are going to get it. Unfortunately, for most people including myself, this gift of positive focus doesn't come pre-wired. But it is something that you can learn.

My first job out of school was at the local McDonalds restaurant. I was a keen employee, eager to learn, and very hard working. The promotional structure within a fast food chain is such that if you stick around long enough and show an active interest in your development (i.e., you want more money), then promotion to management is inevitable. When I was promoted, I was given various responsibilities, one of which was the safety officer. This role required me to walk around the premises looking for potential hazards and take precautionary measures. Working as a safety officer was a curse and a blessing. It conditioned me to focus on problems, but it also taught me to visualise a solution to the situation before it became too dangerous.

This put me somewhere between our two groups of people. I wasn't a negatively focused worrier, but my job required me to look at my environment in the same way that such a person would. However, putting measures in place to avoid potential hazards required me to focus on a more positive future and take action to achieve it. This was definitely a step in the right direction, but it was still short of the ideal. At this stage, if you had asked me what I wanted out of life, I'd have still given you a list of all the things that I didn't want first.

Back then, I had no idea that my focus was causing me to stagnate and that dwelling on the reality I wanted to change was the glue that held it to me. I was beginning to see possible solutions to my situation, but I was still primarily focused on the past.

Looking back over my life, I know that the transition I made in focus was helped along by various experiences, not least of which was my time as a safety officer. There was still work to be done: I didn't consciously know that I desired a more positive focus, so getting one was slow going.

Today, if you were to ask me whether I'm a positive person, I'd immediately answer "yes". I'd actually struggle to remember a time that I wasn't positively focused. For me, this transition began very gradually. It seemed to be something that I was being subjected to through experience, whether I was aware of it or not, because it was a necessary development towards the actualisation of my life purpose. However, as soon as I consciously recognised the potential of a forward facing positive focus, I very quickly began to explore ways in which I could get one.

Anthony Robbins is perhaps one of the most vocal advocates of the importance of being positively focused. He sums it up beautifully in a metaphor that I have used time and time again on my clients in practically any situation where a shift in focus is required.

"If you try to drive forward looking in the rear view mirror, pretty soon you're going to crash."

This is exactly what most people do. They try to change their lives by focusing on their past, which is a sure-fire recipe for disaster. You get more of what you focus on, so if you're trying, for example, to eliminate debt, then thinking about it, moaning about it, or even being pissed off with it is only going to make it bigger! Focusing on where you want to go is the most important step in creating your own reality. If you don't have a clear image of what you want out of life, then creating one is the first step in the process.

A positive focus on our desired reality is important not only when we're talking about the spiritual laws of creation and magnetism, it's also the basis of countless therapies, particularly in the fields of hypnosis and neuro-linguistic programming (NLP). I've been using hypnosis and NLP on my clients (and myself) for many years. Initially, I was primarily dealing with addictions and phobias, and smoking cessation and weight loss were by far the most common requests, as I am sure countless other therapists will agree. Both of these problems were eliminated in essentially the same way using hypnotic suggestions and NLP strategies. The actual therapy content was always different, but the underlying procedure that created the change in the client was exactly the same. The most important step of that process was to get the client to shift their focus away from what they were trying to quit and fix it on what they were trying to become. We would talk about being a non-smoker as opposed to quitting smoking, going to the gym or enjoying a healthy salad instead of counting calories. Each time, the focus was on the desired outcome. My clients created mental images of a perfect future, and then, we turned up the juice and made that mental image incredibly appealing to their subconscious mind. The emphasis was always on the direction of focus. If they were to move forward in their life, it was essential that they see clearly where they were going without getting distracted by that rear view mirror.

Creating your own reality is exactly the same process. If you want to be a certain way, you need to be able to see yourself that way. If you want to have a certain thing, then you need to be able to visualise what having that thing will be like. In all the years I've been helping people to change their lives, every effective technique I've used had this concept right at its heart. My own big picture was never my experience as a therapist. It always felt as though something else more important was just around the corner. When I found that 'something else', I could clearly see how my experiences had lead me down this path. That 'something else' was a much deeper connection. I developed my own spiritual energy through meditation and became a healer. This, coupled with my experience of hypnosis and NLP, led to a thorough understanding of the nature of creation—particularly the way people create their own reality. It came as no surprise that one of the most fundamental ingredients to successful creation was a positive focus on what one wanted to create.

One of the indications of this shift of focus that I noticed in myself was an evident change in my language. I was always hideously pre-occupied with the past and had absolutely no concept of the future what-so-ever. If a friend asked if I wanted to go out at the weekend, I simply couldn't answer; it just seemed like it was so far away that making plans was pointless. My rather frustrating reply became the standard, 'Ask me on Friday'. Similarly, I'd talk of the distant past as though it'd just happened. I constantly used the phrase, 'the other day' when referring to experiences that sometimes went back years. This warped perception of time exposed my own distorted internal representation of reality and holding on to this model was seriously stifling my ability to create the things that I desired. In order to shift my focus, I first needed to adjust my…

Timeline

Your timeline is simply the order in which you perceive the events in your life. Try imagining something that you do every day, such as cleaning your teeth. You'll notice that each representation of this act has its own location within your imagination. For example, if it is this morning you are remembering, you will probably see the image very clearly and quite close to your head. If it is yesterday's instance, the image might be slightly off to the left or maybe behind you, and tomorrow's imagined instance of cleaning your teeth would probably be found off in the respective opposite direction. The further in time you go, the farther away from you the image usually appears. You may also notice other changes, such as a lack of clarity or blurring which increases as the images appear further away.

These are standard examples of timelines. We all use them without any conscious awareness, and they help us to plan future events and create possible future realities. My timeline, however, wasn't like this. The past was very close to me, even events that happened 10 or 15 years ago. And the future... that wasn't anywhere! I couldn't see a future; I could just see fog. If I tried to imagine a future event, nothing came. As a therapist, I've worked with other people's timelines frequently; manipulating the timeline, or even dipping into it can be incredibly therapeutic, especially when resolving past trauma. What I'd noticed was how easily people were able to change when they had a timeline that clearly and logically represented their future.

Your timeline isn't set in stone; it's something that you can very easily play around with. By making adjustments to your timeline, you can change the way you feel about different events in your life. If you're the kind of person that always dwells on the past and finds it hard to let go of emotionally charged memories, then you can literally put the past behind you. My timeline had no future, so I found many of the meditations that required me to focus on my future reality almost impossible.

To adjust your timeline, all you need to do is imagine that you are floating up out of yourself and seeing your timeline in its entirety from above, like a series of photographs. You can then very easily move them around until it's more to your liking. Once you've fiddled with it a bit, drop back down into yourself, and see how the changes have affected the way you think. If you're happy with the changes, keep them. If not, imagine floating back up again, and make further adjustments until you are happy. Changing the way your mind automatically perceives reality just requires a little imagination. As you begin to play with these suggestions, you might find that your mind tries to resist, and you snap back into your old pattern. To overcome this, you simply need to make the change again. After you have gone through the process a few times, your mind seems to recognise what you are trying to do and begins to play ball. From this point on, the new pattern becomes the standard and begins to feel much more natural.

adjust your timeline by floating up. Then bring your future want to your present feeling.

If there is something that you desire, being able to picture yourself having it in the future will increase the possibility of getting it. As you imagine the location of this image on your timeline, you can begin to move things around a little to make it appear closer to you. This makes it feel more real. The more realism you put into your imagination, the more powerful it becomes. Moving the things that you desire through your timeline helps you to determine how comfortable you are about receiving them. As you move something closer to you in time, you might find that your anxiety about owning it increases, indicating that obtaining this item so quickly may cause difficulties—perhaps highlighting things that must be done before you obtain it.

Similarly, moving a desired object closer to you on your timeline can substantially increase your emotional attachment to it. This, as you will see later, will have a massive impact on the speed at which you manifest something you desire in your life. Perhaps the best way to illustrate this is to imagine how you might feel as a child waiting for your birthday. With a timeline that is too foggy to see a future, your excitement about the birthday wouldn't begin until it was almost upon you. But with a timeline that brings the future very close, the excitement begins very early.

As children, my friends all counted the days to their next birthday and eagerly awaited their presents. I could count the days from my previous birthday and tell you exactly how old I was, but the excitement of presents rarely began until much closer to the big day. As I grew up, my blurred perception of the future meant that I was always late for appointments and never, ever completed work on time. Deadlines seemed to be a distant blur right up until the night before they were due. I was constantly accused of procrastinating at school and work, but I wasn't putting things off; I just didn't see any reason to complete tasks immediately when they had no perceivable deadline. Making adjustments to my timeline had a huge impact on my life because my pre-wired model was so impractical. But more importantly, it enabled me to begin to focus on my future.

For the first time in my life, I could see the future and even bring it right up close. This ability made visualisation much easier, and I was finally able to effectively use the manifestation meditations that I knew would help change my life. I urge you to play with your own timeline. Have some fun moving things around and see what you come up with. There is no reason that you should simply accept the model you were born with. It may have served you very well in the past, but it might now be time for a change.

Using your timeline to image your desired future reality is only the first step of the creation process. You really need to bring that visualisation all the way back to the present, so that you feel as though you actually have it now. For many people, trying to feel as though they already have what they want is difficult because their imagined experience is in conflict with their perception of their current reality. Playing with your timeline can help you to bring things closer gradually so that you become more comfortable with them over time.

Because your timeline positions your remembered or imagined experiences in a logical order, you can easily determine the location of the present. This enables you to move your creative visualisations to that location and trick your subconscious mind into believing that you already have them. When your subconscious mind believes something is real, it causes you to send out the spiritual vibration needed to draw that very thing into your life.

As you do visualisation meditations to help magnetise the reality you desire, become aware of their perceived location and compare this to your timeline. Many people automatically and unconsciously place the reality they are trying to manifest in the wrong location. If you are trying to create something in your life, you need to imagine that you have it now, not in the future. Your subconscious mind is very specific when it comes to creating your reality. You get exactly what you focus on, and if your creative visualisations are positioned in a place that your subconscious mind reserves for the future, they will always be in the future. As you progress through time, creative visualisations that you have positioned in the future do not naturally find their way into your present; they remain in the future as something you are always aspiring to become, but never quite managing to realise.

This process can be incredibly frustrating. Your desires are always just around the next corner, so close, but forever out of reach. If you are living such a reality or know someone that is, then you'll recognise some revealing qualities that accompany such a system. Firstly, you'll be incredibly optimistic about your future—totally convinced that everything's going to work out just right. You'll have believed this for as long as you can remember, and even though you are getting older, this wonderful reality doesn't seem to be getting any closer. This is the curse of the dreamers. They go through life totally convinced of their abundant future, but it never manifests. Unfortunately, believing your future will be incredibly abundant means that you do little in the present to help the situation. Dreamers 'know' it's all going to work out fine, so they rarely take action to guarantee that it does.

If this is your natural focus, you'll most likely have found that you had very little to worry about in your younger years, but as you age, you are becoming increasingly desperate to find whatever it is that is going to bring this perceived abundant future reality into your present.

The famous Derek Trotter line, "This time next year we'll be millionaires!" (from the UK sitcom 'Only fools and horses') is a typical example of this creative process in action. By focusing on an abundant future, you are actually creating a present of lack. This is a

34

form of wanting for something, and the process itself actually pushes the desired reality further away from you. We'll be covering this in much more detail later when we look at the ways in which people self-sabotage their success because of misplaced focus. In order to experience your desires now, you need to move your creative visualisation to the location that your 'now' experience naturally resides.

Focusing on a desired reality in such a way as to trick your subconscious mind into thinking it's real is one of the most essential and powerful steps to creating your own reality. There are many simple processes, such as manipulating your timeline, that substantially increase your ability to manifest the things that you want in your life. As a hypnotist, my primary focus when helping clients in any situation is to create a convincing reality of their desired outcome and present it to their subconscious mind in such a way that it's accepted as true. If I can do this effectively, I know that the client will respond well to the therapy.

Focus, as we have already established, is incredibly important in the creative process. Many of the techniques you'll learn throughout this book are ways that you can manipulate your focus so that it is conducive to positive change. The techniques, as you'll discover, are astonishingly simple, but incredibly effective. Their perceived simplicity is often enough to cause readers to neglect their practise. I strongly urge you to apply these principles to your own life. Yes, they are simple, but do not allow this to blind you to their necessity and effectiveness in totally transforming your reality.

To quickly recap: so far, we have established that you need to focus on your desire in order to get it, NOT on what you want to move away from. If you want riches, you must focus on riches. If you want health, then healthy thoughts must occupy your mind. Focusing on the reality you desire is paramount to your success in achieving it. We have also established that manipulating your timeline can make having whatever it is you desire more comfortable. And ultimately, you need to move your creative visualisation to whatever area your mind perceives as the present if you want your desires to become your reality, rather than their forever remaining just out of reach.

Now we need to take...

A Closer Look at Focus

Your focus has many variables. We've already discussed how shifting your focus through time and keeping it positive has a massive effect on your ability to create your own reality. Now, we'll take a look at how manipulating the more subtle variables of focus can make this process much more powerful. This means that you can enjoy whatever reality you desire sooner and much more completely. To put this in simple terms, the better you are able to convince your subconscious mind that whatever you are focusing on is real, the quicker it will manifest in your physical reality and the more accurate it will be. Manipulating the variables of your thoughts changes the way they make you feel, and it is this shift in emotions that really fuels the creative process. If you can become passionate about your desires, then they will very soon be your reality.

What you are about to discover is incredibly simple, yet it is perhaps one of the most powerful techniques you'll ever use to boost your creative abilities. It has the ability to fuel your visualisations with such emotion that you become a spiritual magnet to your desires. This simple technique transforms the way you perceive reality to such an extent that it can completely neutralise a traumatic memory in seconds. This simple, easy-to-use technique that requires very little practice and no tools or previous experience is the backbone of many life changing therapies. If used correctly, it can eliminate a phobia in minutes. Very recently, I used this process on a complete stranger who knew I was a hypnotist and asked if I could hypnotise him sometime to help overcome a childhood trauma. I told him hypnosis wasn't necessary, and I could do the therapy immediately if he was comfortable for me to proceed.

Within minutes, tears of joy rolled down his cheeks as his perception of the experience was totally transformed, freeing him from a lifetime of torment. I use this process with clients all the time. It works so quickly that I find myself padding it out in order to lengthen the session so the client feels as though they've gotten their money's worth. Change can and does happen in an instant, but many people have become so conditioned into believing that it takes time to change that such a powerful, yet simple technique is hard to believe. Before I share this wonderful process with you, I want to make sure that you understand how powerful it is. Don't allow its simplicity to distract you from its effectiveness.

As you read the following paragraphs, you might find yourself thinking, 'Oh! Is that all? I thought this was going to be some miraculous secret that could save the planet!' If you do... Don't! Instead of feeling disappointed that this process is 'so simple it couldn't possibly make that much difference', feel totally elated that this process can and does make that much difference, then become completely ecstatic that it is simple, and allow yourself to overflow with joy when you realise that you can use it to massively boost your creative abilities and have whatever you desire!

If a secret technique exists that can deliver your deepest desires, would you rather it be so bombastic as to completely elude you? Or would you prefer it to be so simple and straight forward that you only need to be shown its utter simplicity once, and you can use it for the rest of your life in countless situations to get whatever you desire? Prefer simple? Excellent! Because as good fortune would have it, such a technique does exist! It's simple, anyone can easily do it, and it's incredibly powerful. So let's have some fun...

Imagine you're watching a roller coaster at the funfair. As you watch the coaster car speed around the track, you suddenly notice it's you in the front seat! Watch yourself on the coaster, right at the front as the car twists, turns, and loops its way through the ride. As you watch the ride come to an end, I want you to very quickly score the ride out of 100. Your score should reflect how exciting the ride felt or how scared you were (depending on how much you enjoy riding coasters!). As soon as you have your score, walk over to the coaster. Watch the 'other you' climb out of the car, and then get in.

Now, you're going to experience the coaster ride again, but this time instead of seeing yourself in the image, you'll see the experience through you own eyes, just as you'd see it in real life. You can hear the clunking of the drive chain as your car begins to slowly make its way skyward, ready for the first big drop. As the car jolts and jerks, you glance over the side. You notice how high you are and feel the final shudder as the car begins to slowly glide onto free track and you teeter at the edge of the first big drop.... While you are holding your breath daring to look down, the car begins to tilt forward, and you feel your body rise in your seat as you're suddenly speeding down a huge vertical drop with the ground rushing towards you....

OK... in your own time, whiz through the rest of the coaster ride making sure you imagine the entire experience as though you were really there. This means you won't see yourself, but you will see everything that you would normally see in real life. It'll help if you stop reading and close your eyes!

Finished? Great! Now mark the experience out of 100. Notice the difference? Both of these scenarios contain exactly the same facts—your riding a coaster. But by changing your perception of the experience, you were able to massively increase the emotions it produced. This is incredibly important because emotions are key to success in manifestation. By using this simple tool that can increase your emotional response to an imagined scenario, you are making manifestation meditations much, much more powerful. This is manifestation turbocharged!

During our little coaster ride, you experience two different perspectives—disassociated and associated. By associating with an imagined experience, you essentially live that experience and your subconscious mind responds as though it's completely real. The more associated you are, the more real the situation becomes and greater the effect it has on your emotions. For example, when people normally imagine riding a coaster in an associated way, they tend to visualise the experience using their imagination to 'see' the ride, just like one of the old 180° cinema screens at the fair that used to make you fall over. But did you imagine the wind on your face, the harness pressing your shoulders or the feeling of the seat beneath you? Could you feel the hot sun shining down on your skin or hear the other riders screaming? The more detail you put into the experience, the more real it becomes. Ideally, you should involve all of your senses, really get into it. Feel exactly how you'd feel, see what you'd see, hear what you'd hear, smell what you'd smell, and taste what you'd taste. Get as involved as possible, just as though you were riding the coaster for real.

When I hypnotise people, I often have to describe realities that they desire to enable them to manifest these realities. In order to do this, I simply describe various aspects of the scene to them involving each of their senses so they can easily recreate it internally. To boost the emotional involvement as much as possible, I really pull out all the stops and make sure they are totally associated with the experience. It also helps to match the experience with my tonality; so if they are riding a coaster, I speak very quickly and sound incredibly excited, but if I want them to relax, I speak much... much...... more... slooooooooowly... as I describe wonderfully relaxing experiences that seduce all of their senses.

By doing the coaster exercise, you can easily see how changing your view point affects your emotions, and as you know, increasing your emotions fools your subconscious mind into believing that you are actually having the experience for real. This is seriously good news because it causes your spiritual energy to resonate at the exact frequency required to bring that experience into your reality.

As you'll discover later, the process of getting something that you want is the emotion of already having it. Now you have a way to access those emotions and crank them right up! All you need to do is imagine that you already have whatever it is you want and make sure you are completely associated with it. Mastering the ability to shift your perception is easy—the tricky part is to remember to do it when it will benefit you, rather than playing out your daydreams (or memories) using whichever system your subconscious mind has automatically selected.

You've already seen how increasing your emotional involvement can assist you in manifesting the reality you desire. Now, you're going to discover how using this process the other way around can help you too. Whenever you recall a memory, depending on the way you think about it, a certain amount of emotion comes back with it. If you remember a situation by totally associating with the experience, it's as though you were actually re-living it. The memory will be overflowing with emotion. If your recalled experience is viewed so that you are able to see yourself in the scene, then you are dissociated, and although you can clearly see the facts of the experience, it's very difficult to get the emotions back that you were experiencing at the time.

So how can this be useful? For your own general well being, it's extremely effective if you only choose to associate with the memories that bring you joyful emotions and disassociate from those that are painful. This is what most happy people do naturally. Depressed people, on the other hand, are the other way around; they tend to completely associate with their negative memories which causes all of the bad feelings to come flooding back. We also get people that associate with everything, and their emotions yo-yo up and down all over the place depending on what it is they are thinking about at the time. Finally, there are those that don't associate with anything at all which makes life kind of dull. This last category is the one that I belonged to before I discovered that I can take control of the process.

For me, moving from a disassociated position to an associated one was like stepping into my own body. I'd initially see the situation in the 'usual' way with a representation of myself 'over there' having the experience as I looked on from the sidelines. All I had to do to switch the situation was to walk over and imagine stepping into that other me. To make this easier, I imagined that the other version of me had a zipper running all the way down their back. I'd pull the zipper down and then literally step inside, as though putting on an all-in-one boiler suit. I'd imagine my hands sliding into theirs like a pair of gloves and then completely align myself inside so that I could see through their eyes, smell using their nose, hear with their ears and feel everything they felt. At this point,

I simply became that person and was totally associated with the experience.

If I wanted to disassociate from an experience, I'd imagine floating upwards and backwards right out of myself until I felt totally disconnected from the other me that I left in place. Disassociating in this way really helps to reduce your emotional response to the experience. However, sometimes, such as when dealing with a phobia or traumatic memory, you need to take that disassociated feeling a step further. This is where you repeat the process on your disassociated self so you imagine floating up out of yourself twice. This leaves you in a position where you are watching a 2nd version of you looking at a 3rd version of you having an experience. It sounds complicated to explain, but to actually do it is very simple.

[handwritten margin note: think only Positive. Eliminate bad Memories by backing out of yourself & let your shell self stay w/the bad Memory.]

Getting back to creating your own reality, you'll primarily be working with developing your associated viewpoint so that you can make your manifestation meditations as real as possible. However, until you have conditioned your mind to be positive, you can also make use of the disassociated perspective to remove emotions from imagined experiences that might create a reality you do not desire. For example, if you have a lot of debt, ideally you'll want to focus on having abundance and completely associate with the experience. However, if you find yourself focused on the debt as you crunch figures with your financial advisor, you can disassociate your emotions from the experience but still get the work done.

What you're striving for is to become completely focused on the positive aspects of where you want to go and to make them as real as possible. As you practise using these techniques and develop your skills, your subconscious mind will soon get the hang of it, and much of this will happen automatically.

Before we move on, would you also like to possess skills that you admire in others? I'd like to share with you a very powerful technique that makes use of association to enable you to develop such skills. First of all, think of a skill or quality that you'd like to have—it can be anything at all. You might choose to be more confident, to be more charismatic, or perhaps, you'd just like to improve your golf swing.

Next, imagine someone that already has this quality or skill and visualise them in your mind for a few moments. If you can't think of a real person, you can make one up... or even use a cartoon super hero if it's appropriate! Spend a few moments watching as they perform in the way that you would like to. Imagine that you are actually in the scene too, but be sure you are seeing everything as though you were really there. You need to be fully associated into the experience, so it's important that you can't see yourself walking around.

who has completely retired and is enjoying life? do this.

Now, pause the entire scene so that the other person you are admiring freezes in place. Walk up behind them. Imagine a zipper running down their back, open it up, and step inside. Just as we did previously, step right into that person as though you were putting on a boiler suit. Slide your hands into theirs and totally associate with the experience that they are having. Once you're completely inside them, use your imagination to feel everything, exactly as they feel it. If they wear glasses, feel the frames resting on your nose. Feel the material of their clothes on your skin. Feel, see, hear, smell and taste everything exactly as they would. Even imagine that you speak, move, and think like they do!

Now, un-pause the scene, and with yourself completely associated with the experience, allow them to continue performing as before. Enjoy this experience for as long as you are comfortable before you float back out of the person and thank them for assisting you. Then simply open your eyes and bring your awareness back here. This technique is called modelling, and you can use it to learn absolutely anything. If you can imagine someone else doing something, then you can step right into that person and learn how to do it yourself. You might like to try stepping inside some of the people that truly inspire you, such as Anthony Robbins or Deepak Chopra. Or perhaps you fancy having a go inside Madonna!

This process makes focusing on what you desire in an associated way much easier and far more realistic as you tend to feel much less resistance to the process than you would by simply imagining yourself in the situation, especially if it's very different from your current experience. For example, if you are currently struggling to pay the bills and you try to focus on abundance, you might find your conflicting thoughts about your current situation interfere with your success. But if you just think of a person that has more money than they could possibly ever spend and step into their body, you can enjoy all of the feelings that this experience brings you without conflict. The emotions that such an experience creates are the key to unlock that exact experience in your life!

Stepping into people is fun; enjoy the experience and play with it often. You should view this technique as a game, just like playing dress-up as a child. These techniques are fun games that have massive rewards, not exercises that you need to struggle with to try and get what you want. Take time out everyday to really enjoy being someone else for a few minutes. As you allow the emotions of the experience to flow, you are sending out an incredibly powerful spiritual vibration that attracts these qualities into your life. Modelling other people helps you to lay down new and more empowering beliefs, which is a really valuable tool because…

Your Beliefs Create Your Reality

When the friend I introduced you to earlier told me about his vision of the future, the reality he described wasn't some unachievable pipe dream. It was a realistic possibility that he whole heartedly believed he could achieve. The future he envisaged was very different to the reality he was experiencing at the time, but he knew it was obtainable. He didn't know how, but he knew it was possible.

Our beliefs play an important role in our ability to manipulate the future. If we can imagine a future that we believe in, we are much more likely to be able to create it as our reality. If we do not believe in the future we imagine for ourselves, it will take longer and be substantially more difficult to achieve. That said, it's important you understand that you don't need to believe your cosmic orders to get them, but if you do, it will make things happen much quicker! As you begin using these techniques, you may find it difficult to believe that they work, but you'll soon overcome this resistance as you begin to see the results for yourself.

Beliefs are incredibly powerful things; some are obvious, but many are hidden in the depths of your subconscious mind. Some beliefs can be particularly troublesome when you are trying to change your reality, and you need to weed them out in order to enjoy the most favourable results from your efforts.

If you believe that you get more of what you focus on and you recognise that you tend to focus on what you believe, then you'll appreciate the huge impact that your beliefs have on your reality. Your beliefs are currently dictating your life, so if you want your life to change, you need to start by changing your beliefs. If you imagine that your life is a garden, your social standing, hobbies, personality traits, possessions, and well-being are the flowers and weeds that grow in that garden. All of this stuff is above ground. Anyone wandering through your garden can easily see them. It goes without saying that the gardens of some people are in desperate need of a make-over, whereas others are beautifully stocked with exotic flowers and neatly trimmed lawns.

If you have something in your life that you're not completely happy with, you'll be able to locate a weed in this garden that represents the situation. It might be the state of your finances, a bad habit or addiction, or perhaps a phobia. This weed could have been around for many years, and you may have tried to remove it several times, but it just keeps on coming back. Going beneath the surface of the soil, you'll find a network of roots (your subconscious) that support the plants above. The seeds (your beliefs) too from which these roots grew are beneath the surface; you can't normally see them. However, the nature of the plants (your experiences) in your garden is more than enough to know which seeds are there. If there is an oak tree in your garden, then there had to be an acorn beneath the soil from which it grew. The acorn absolutely had to be there; otherwise, the oak tree would simply never exist.

The only difference between a real garden and the reality of your experience is that the seed continues to exist beneath the surface in the latter case. Setting aside the root network for the moment, if you want to remove the oak from your garden, you must remove the acorn beneath the surface. Cutting down the oak will not help because, as long as the acorn exists, the tree will grow back. But if the acorn is removed, the tree will very rapidly die. That's the reality of the relationship between the beliefs that are hidden in your subconscious mind (the acorn) and your experience of reality (the oak tree). Likewise, for you to change your reality, you need to identify the beliefs in your subconscious that create it. If you are in debt, you will definitely have at least one belief that supports and indeed creates this reality. If you find yourself trapped in an endless cycle of failed relationships, then somewhere beneath the surface is a seed that makes this happen.

It's important to remember that these beliefs are beneath the surface. You can't normally see them, so it's safe to assume that you might be surprised at what you find when you look underground. It's great fun to look at the gardens of people you know and work out which seeds must be beneath the surface of their garden, given the plants that are growing up top. For example, if you know someone that seems to win everything, they probably have one or more beliefs supporting (and creating) this reality for them, such as 'I'm really lucky', or 'I'm better than everyone else', or maybe 'I'm a winner'.

Think of the effect of these beliefs literally: if you plant an 'I'm a winner' seed in your garden, it's going to grow into an 'I'm a winner' plant! If you have lots of such seeds, then you'll have an impressive display of 'I'm a winner' plants, and the people that stroll through your garden will most definitely be aware of them. Some of those people will admire your display, others will be a little jealous, and some might even ask you for a cutting so that they can grow their own.

Whatever beliefs you hold on to grow into your reality. Not creating your own reality is completely impossible. However, it often seems as though you were not the creator, especially when the reality you are experiencing is so far from the one that you desire. In fact, this is true in one sense. While you create your reality based on what you believe, your beliefs are rarely your own creation. Almost everything you believe will have been influenced by others, so if your beliefs are not your own, someone else is dictating your life. It's about time that you took back control.

Many of the beliefs that could be holding you back from experiencing the life you desire have probably been with you since childhood. As children, we are very receptive to suggestion due to the absence of something called the critical factor. The critical factor can be thought of as a guardian that protects the passage that connects the conscious and subconscious minds. In our garden analogy, the critical factor is the groundskeeper that stops you planting new seeds or removing existing ones.

As children, this guardian of the mind is absent, so most of the suggestions that we receive are simply accepted without question. The source of the suggestion, the way it is actually suggested, the mood we are in at the time, and the number of times we hear it are all factors that influence whether or not a particular suggestion makes it through to our subconscious mind to form a part of our belief system. For example, if you are told that you are worthless by your parents or school teachers over and over again, it's pretty safe to assume that you'll start to believe it at a subconscious level and begin to feel worthless.

Consciously, you won't know why you feel this way, and you might not even be aware that you actually feel it at all, but it will show in things that you do. If you later start your own business, you'll probably feel uncomfortable charging your clients the going rate for your services.

What has happened here is that a 'you are worthless' seed has been (perhaps inadvertently) planted in your subconscious mind and it has grown into an aspect of your reality, growing plants like 'lower prices' (actions that confirm 'you are worthless'). Without the seed, the plant cannot exist.

When you try to uproot the plant, your subconscious mind will do all it can to protect the seed even if it is not for your greater good. It will concoct an assortment of reasons to explain your actions and avoid exposing the hidden belief. You might explain your reduced prices as generosity, a desire to make your products available to those on low incomes, or maybe as a strategy to attract more sales, ultimately generating more profit. There will be many examples that your subconscious mind will present to you as reasons for your actions, and each of these will help to mask the belief of worthlessness.

Obviously, there are many reasons that a person may lower their prices, and not all of these will stem from a negative or disempowering subconscious belief. To identify the ones that do, you need only to look at the explanations your subconscious mind presents to you as reasons for your actions. Those that hide negative or disempowering beliefs will feel like excuses, and when you think of them you'll feel bad. However, those that support positive empowering beliefs will feel like reasons, and when you think of these, you'll feel good.

The guardian that prevents new beliefs from gaining access to your subconscious mind doesn't actually take up position until around the onset of puberty. So for the first twelve or so years of your life, you have been subjected to a barrage of suggestions that have created the basis of your belief system. Not all of those suggestions are still active; some were replaced or upgraded as you learned greater truths from more credible sources.

Once the critical factor is in place, without the right techniques or know-how, it's actually very difficult to consciously change your belief structure. This is the reason that people suffer from irrational phobias. Conventional reasoning is a conscious process. In our garden, it happens above the surface. We can reason with a troublesome weed until we are blue in the face, but it isn't going to make any difference. However, if we pull out all the stops and attack the weed with will power, reasoning, motivation, and whatever else we have in our conscious arsenal of transformation, we can remove a weed from the garden. But we are still only tackling what we can see above the surface; if the roots and seeds of belief are still in place beneath the surface, it won't be long before the weed is back. If you have ever struggled to give up a bad habit and failed, this is what you were going through. You probably beat yourself up for failing, but in reality, you deserve commendation for your efforts. You took on the awesome power of your subconscious mind single handed, and even if you were only victorious for a few days, you should count this as a triumphant victory. You fought a formidable opponent and won a battle.

Your subconscious mind may have fought back, so your victory, even for sometime, was certainly no easy feat. The goal isn't to beat your subconscious mind; that's never going to happen. The goal is to get it on your side, and to do this, you need to delve a little deeper and make changes where it really matters. This is what happens when you delve beneath the surface and attack the seed and roots that support a weed. They give the weed life. You don't need to focus on the weed at all; just remove the seed and roots that feed it, and it will die all by itself.

To make this kind of change, you need a strategy that enables you to bypass the critical factor so you can remove any bad seeds supporting the weeds that plague your garden. There are several ways that you can do this: hypnosis and NLP are probably the most common and effective ways to bypass the critical factor, but there are many others too. Before you begin exploring your subconscious mind and weeding out anything that doesn't serve you, it's time to recognise that you very probably carry numerous beliefs that simply aren't true! Some of these will be substantially affecting your experience of reality. They will be putting false ceilings on your achievements and stifling your potential in a way that will seem criminal when they are exposed. They'll hide behind numerous excuses and desperately try to support their distorted version of reality with a string of examples that appear to validate their existence.

Once a belief is rooted in your subconscious, it pulls out all the stops to ensure it stays put. Your perception of reality is filtered so that you expose yourself to only those things that support the belief. You attract other people that share a similar belief and happily exchange examples of validation. You are easily able to picture past events that are in alignment with the belief, and anything that conflicts with it is either ignored or dismissed.

Your subconscious mind is incredibly aware of reality, yet it brings things to your attention only if it considers that they will be of interest to you. Every so often, you'll notice this process in action. Perhaps, the most notable example is something called the cocktail syndrome. This is when you hear someone say your name across a noisy room even though you could not consciously hear anything else that was being said by that person. Your subconscious mind was monitoring every conversation going on, and when it heard your name, it alerted you as it assumed it would be something that you needed to hear. It's this same process that exposes you only to events that support your distorted perception of reality.

Your subconscious mind shields you from anything that conflicts with your beliefs and brings those things that support your beliefs into your conscious awareness. Obviously, given that your experience of reality is just a fraction of the real thing, and your subconscious mind filters your perception in alignment with your current beliefs, it would be beneficial for you to remove any beliefs that might encourage your subconscious mind to present you with a negative reality and install some positive beliefs that will encourage you to experience a more desirable slice of what is available.

The reality of creation actually goes much deeper than mere perception. Your beliefs not only dictate the way you perceive reality, they also dictate the reality itself. However, for you to actually create a desired reality rather than just a perception of one, you need more than a belief to support it. This is evident in talent shows when contestants wholeheartedly believe that they have what it takes to be the next superstar, yet we can all clearly see that what they actually have is a grossly distorted perception of their own talent! To change their reality, not just their perception of it, requires a few more manifestation tricks that we'll be looking into later. We're going to focus on beliefs for a while first as a good belief structure is the foundation of change and will really help to support some of the other techniques required to create the reality you desire and prevent you from reverting back to your old patterns in the future.

Many people jump straight into cosmic creation without working on their belief structure first. This is fine for manifesting the odd item that you desire, but it does have its drawbacks. You are constantly in the process of creating your reality; when you are not doing so consciously, you are doing so unconsciously. The problem arises when the blueprint of creation that your subconscious mind follows isn't what you desire, and that blueprint is automatically created based on your beliefs and focus. This means that if you address the problem areas first, then you'll naturally go through life creating everything you desire with no need for conscious effort at all. You'll also enjoy much greater success when you create consciously. You can achieve this by simply...

Conditioning Your Beliefs

There are various techniques you can use to change what you currently believe in order to create a more positive blueprint for your subconscious mind to follow. Try out all of the suggestions, and use those that you are most comfortable with. People think in different ways, so what works for one person might not be suitable for someone else. You might also find that different techniques suit different situations, so really play with them and enjoy whatever happens. The most important thing to remember is to have fun; if you approach these exercises as though they were little games you can play, you'll enjoy much more favourable results. Keep it light hearted and mess around. Mix things up if you want to, and don't be afraid to make up your own strategies using those given as inspiration. Before we get into the actual techniques you'll be using, I want to explore a couple of reasons that may have made manifestation exercises difficult for you in the past.

As already stated, we don't all think alike, so when you try to do an exercise that was designed by someone that doesn't share your methods of thinking, it's often very difficult to follow. Luckily, there are only a handful of variations in the way we process information, and there are some fantastic techniques for changing your belief structure in all of them! So whatever system you use, you'll be able to find a strategy that works for you. Although we are not confined to a single way of thinking, we do tend to favour some over others, and we use different ones in different situations. These varying ways of thinking are called modalities.

The main ones you'll be using are visualisation, auditory processing, and kinaesthetic sensations. You'll already have your favourite. I personally prefer to think using the auditory system, but I also use the other two regularly as well. Ideally, your manifestation meditations should include all three systems, as well as the less commonly used senses of taste and smell, if appropriate. The sense of smell can be particularly powerful and is often overlooked when working on manifestation techniques.

Perhaps, the most commonly used modality is visualisation, and in many ways, it's also one of the most useful. But if this isn't your preferred system or you find visualisation difficult, don't worry; you're in exactly the same position that I was! Natalie (my partner) is primarily visual, and it's very apparent when she is speaking. Visual people tend to use a lot of visual references, such as 'I see what you mean' or 'That looks great!' They also make lots of hand gestures, as though drawing pictures in the air. One of the great things about thinking in a visual way is the huge amount of information that you can process in one go. Information is processed in pictures, so you see images in your mind that can contain lots of detail in a flash.

This also has its problems! Many visual thinkers are mistakenly labelled as air heads! They spend a lot of time day dreaming and can easily become so engrossed in their own internal imagery that the outside world fades completely out of perception. Another common and often amusing trait of the visual thinker is stumbling over their words, especially when they're excited! Because information is presented as an image internally, they have a lot of detail to get out. The humble voice with its linear limitations can't handle such a rush of data in one go, and the result is often a babble of confusion that makes no sense to anybody.

However, visual thinkers make great spellers; they see a word written out in their mind before they use it. I'm a terrible speller because my auditory system says the word in my mind and words are very rarely spelt the way they sound. By developing my own visualisation skills, I was able to improve my spelling considerably. Now, I can imagine a word visually and instantly know if it looks right.

Perhaps, the second most popular modality is the one I tend to favour—auditory. This is thinking in sounds. People that use this system will make many auditory references during conversation, such as 'That sounds great' or 'Her name rings a bell.' Because auditory thinkers think in pretty much the same way that we usually converse, everything moves along at a much slower pace compared to visual thinkers. Auditory thinkers make great musicians and can be very chatty, but they do value their silence! Too much noise can be incredibly irritating, and loud noises are actually painful. As an auditory thinker, you'll spend a lot of time engaged in internal dialogue. Other people will probably see subtle movements in your lips as you do this, and you'll often adopt an 'on the phone' posture without realising it. When a person is deeply engaged in the auditory modality, they'll often start talking to themselves, probably even without realising it, so we do sometimes get labelled 'a little eccentric!'

Third on our list, we have kinaesthetic thinkers. These people are incredibly in touch with their physical being and emotions; they think by feeling and will trust their gut instinct over everything. A kinaesthetic thinker needs to tune into their own body to really 'grasp' how they 'feel' about a situation. If you ask them a question, you can expect a short pause before a reply as this 'going inside' process takes time. They also tend to look down a lot as this is the position our eyes naturally move to as we access our feelings. This obviously means they need to break eye contact regularly, and when the reply comes, it's being permanently monitored by their feelings, so it comes slowly. Of the three main types of thinkers, the kinaesthetic thinker communicates considerably slower than the others. All of this is often perceived as a lack of intelligence by the visually rich world of the media. As a result, many incredibly gifted athletes often wrongfully gain the reputation of being somewhat stupid.

Communication between two people that are using different systems can be very frustrating. A visual thinker will be loud and talk quickly; a kinaesthetic thinker will perceive this as untrustworthy and prefer a mellower pace. Unfortunately, the visual thinker will become frustrated and bored with the slooooooow pace of the kinaesthetic and try to speed things up even more!

When you break down each modality into its subcomponents, you have what we call submodalities. These are the variable qualities of each system. For example, the submodalities of the visual system include colour, brightness, focus, and contrast. The auditory system has pitch, pace, and volume, and the kinaesthetic system has weight, temperature, and texture. Obviously, there are many more definitions for each, but these are the basics. Manifestation meditations make liberal use of the manipulation of these submodalities to enable you to massively increase your magnetic powers. So if you take a little time working with them, you'll get whatever you desire much quicker! Although it isn't necessary, you can enjoy more favourable results from your meditations if you first put a little effort into developing your inner senses. As I am primarily an auditory thinker, I tend to hear a lot of voices in my head, I run through imaginary conversations regularly, and I have a good ear for music. These skills are very useful in certain areas of my life: I play the drums and guitar, so they most certainly help out there. When I first began playing the guitar, I noticed how tuning by ear helped to develop my perception of sound so that I was able to distinguish subtle variations in pitch much more clearly. This later proved very useful in my meditations.

Throughout my childhood, I was always a very keen artist. I regularly enjoyed drawing or painting what I could see, but I found drawing from memory very difficult. Focusing on visualisation skills helped me to develop a more vivid imagination. This made drawing much easier; I no longer needed to be looking at something to draw it. I could just draw from memory or make things up as I went along. Many architects have an incredible ability to construct their designs mentally before even putting pen to paper. This is a skill I recognised in others and wanted to develop for myself. Developing my visualisation skills was one of the most useful things I ever did. I originally found visualisation incredibly difficult, but it soon became second nature.

As most meditations use visualisation techniques, I often found them frustrating. This is the problem that a lot of people experience when trying to work on pre-scripted meditations. Originally, I designed my own variations of meditations that enabled me to stick with my preferred auditory system, but as my visualisation skills developed, I began to work with a combination of the two and found the meditations much more powerful. The third big player, kinaesthetic, is the one that completely eluded me! I had very little awareness of my body and not a great deal of control over it. I also found it very difficult to access my feelings and never experienced much variation in emotion whatsoever. Developing your ability to feel is incredibly important. Many advanced meditations only work if you are expressing love as you do them. To assist in developing this feeling, I held a picture, such as a kitten, in my mind that enabled me to experience loving emotions. This technique proved particularly useful as I was also able to imagine holding the kitten in my hands and feeling its soft warm fur.

Developing your inner senses enables you to construct an internal reality that works like a blueprint. Once you have a clear internal blueprint to follow, it becomes much easier for your subconscious mind to actualise your desires. When you focus on what you want to create, you should be as precise as you can. Remember that cosmic ordering is very much like making a telephone call; if you want to talk to a specific person, you need to dial the correct number. So if you want to create a specific thing, you need to make a specific blueprint with your internal senses. The more realistic you can make this internal representation, the more effective your meditations will be. By developing your inner senses, you can make things seem as real to your subconscious mind as anything that you have experienced in the physical world.

In addition to developing your internal senses, you can also make use of eye movements to kick start a particular modality that you want to use. Our eyes naturally move to different locations depending on which modality we are using as we think. If we are thinking visually, we tend to look up, although some people that are very good at visualisation often simply stare straight ahead. Whether our eyes go up and left or up and right will depend on whether we are remembering something we have already seen or constructing something new. Most people look up and to the right if they are creating images in their mind, and this is the archetypical 'day dreamer' pose.

You can test this yourself with a partner. Simply ask them a question that requires them to remember a visual image in order to answer, such as the colour of their front door. In order to access the information needed to answer this question, they will have to see an image from their memory, and their eyes will probably go up and to the left to access it. If you ask a question that requires some creative visualisation, such as what a bright green elephant would look like, their eyes will probably move up and to the right. The same happens with remembering or creating internal sounds; however, rather than looking up we tend to look to the side—usually left to remember and right to create. If we are engaged in internal dialogue, we usually look down and to the left, and for accessing our feelings, our eyes will move down and right. When engaged in self dialogue, it's very common to touch your mouth or stroke your chin; this is a very typical thinking pose and is beautifully illustrated by Rodin's 'Thinker' sculpture.

Not everyone's eye will follow this pattern; you might have your own unique pattern, so it's important to determine where your eyes go when you think in different ways if you want to use the process effectively. Once you know which direction your eyes move for each system, you can use the process in reverse. This is like pushing a manual car so that the wheels start the engine. If you need to create a visual image, then you'll find it easier if you look up and right; if you need to remember one then look up left. This is a great way to help develop your ability to create your internal reality. You can work in each modality to create a thoroughly rich environment that looks, sounds, and feels completely real.

The real beauty of your internal creations begins when you start to manipulate the submodalities, and it is by doing this that you can begin to change your belief system to support the reality that you desire. The submodalities of our internal representation of experience are like unique codes, each one created from a combination of variables that work just like a recipe. The trick is to identify which codes are used in different situations so that you can apply them where necessary in order to make your visualisations more believable, and the easiest way to visualise this process is to think of your imagination as a TV program. The modalities used in the program are visual (the picture on the screen) and auditory (the sound); the submodalities are the qualities of those things. Your TV remote control enables you to change many of these, such as the volume, contrast, brightness, and colour, very easily. There are other submodalities too, such as the size of the screen and its location in relation to you.

The screen might be very big and close or perhaps really tiny and far away. All of these variations have an effect on the way you perceive the program. Close your eyes for a few moments and think of a person that you truly love. With your eyes closed, reach out your hand and touch their face; then open your eyes and note the position of your hand.

Next, close your eyes and think of a person that you hate. Again reach out and touch their face; then open your eyes and note the position of you hand in relation to the person you love. Thirdly, close your eyes and think of a person that you barely know, someone for whom you have no feelings whatsoever. Reach out to touch their face; then open your eyes to check the position of your hand. Most people will find that all three images appear in different spatial locations. The third one is often much further away from your face than the first two, and the first one is usually the closest.

What you are revealing here is the way that your emotional attachment to each person affects one of the sub-modalities (location) of your inner vision. You might find that the first two people appear in the same location or very close to one another. This often happens because, although you love one and hate the other, both of these are very powerful emotions. If these perceived images are very close to you in relation to the third image, it would be safe to say that you store internal images of things that you have a strong emotional attachment to very close to you, whereas those things that you only have a weak emotional attachment to are perceived as being further away.

Whether you are working with visual images, sounds, or feelings, the location sub-modality is usually the one that has the largest impact on the way you feel about something. So discovering how different spatial locations affect you is very important. By changing the natural location of a perceived image in your mind, you can change the way you feel about it. The first time you do this, it feels weird; as you move the image to a new location, it feels out of place and very quickly snaps back to its original position. However if you persist, very soon the image will stay in the new location, and the way you feel about whatever it is changes accordingly.

When you are moving images around in your mind this way, it sometimes helps to actually move them with your physical hands. Reach out and imagine you are grabbing hold of the image you want to move. Slide it to its new location, and hold it there for a while. You might even like to click it in place with an imagined sound. The snapping sound that a plastic lid makes when you close a container is great for this. When you let go, if it slides back, grab it again and move it back until it remains in place. Manipulating the location of your visualisations can substantially increase your ability to create your desired reality because you can simply move everything that you want to have to the location that your mind automatically puts things that you already have. This will make you feel as though you already have them and cause your spiritual vibration to resonate at the same frequency as your desired outcome, which attracts it to you. Moving images around is incredibly effective. As a therapist, I use this technique in all kinds of situations. Perhaps, the most interesting is to help people to lose weight.

Overweight people often have a specific problem—food that they eat far too much of and far too often. Even when they are not eating it, they are thinking about it. In many cases, this is simply due to the location that the representation of that particular food item (lets call it chocolate cake) has in their mind. Chocolate cake (if you eat too much of it) appears very close; it's usually very big, the image is rich in colour, and it comes complete with a gorgeous chocolaty aroma. Because it's right up in their face, they think about it a lot and because it looks so tempting, smells so scrumptious, and makes your mouth water as it tantalises your taste buds…they eat it…a lot! The trick, as I am sure you've already guessed (that's if you are still reading and not off raiding the larder for chocolate cake!!), is to move that image away. As it moves further from their face, it loses its alluring qualities and suddenly doesn't seem so appealing. To make it even duller, you can drain out all colour, switch off the smell, and shrink down the image. If you want to pull out all the stops, you can imagine a small frame around the cake, so it now appears as an old tattered black and white photograph. Now, imagine you are in a long corridor. Walk to the end, stick the photograph on the wall, then turn around and walk away from it. Once you are back here with me, turn and look at the cake all the way over there. Notice how it's suddenly not that tempting any more?

As useful as this may sound, it's only half of the process. As we already know, whatever you focus on you get more of, so even though the cake's appeal has substantially diminished, it's still the object of our focus. Therefore, we need to put something else in its way. If I'm working with a client that needs more exercise, then I create a mental image of them really enjoying a great workout. We dress up this new image with all the submodalities it needs to make it irresistibly appealing, then stick it right in front of their face. If the client needs to eat healthier food, then we create an image of that too and juice it up so it's good enough to eat.

This is what I call the submodality diet. It works because it changes the way you feel about food so that you don't want to eat all those unhealthy goodies. Instead, you exercise lots and eat the good stuff because when you think about it, it just looks so appealing! The great thing about this diet is that it enables you to eat anything you want to eat, which means you no longer feel as though you're missing out or suffering. The only thing that changes is the things that you actually want or don't want to eat in the first place! 'Denial diets' (that's the type that most people use) are ongoing self torture and more frustratingly, they don't really work!

Aside of keeping your figure in check and prolonging your life, you can also use this simple process to change your beliefs. Just as your perception of chocolate cake has different submodalities to your perception of sprouts, your perception of things that you truly believe will be different to your perception of those you'd like to believe but don't. Just to mix things up a little, this time we are going to explore the auditory system and investigate ways that you can fiddle with the sounds in your head to really believe something that you currently don't. Remember, your beliefs are like seeds that grow into your reality, so by planting some really empowering beliefs you are paving the way for a truly abundant and joyful future!

It's worth noting that you're very probably not currently experiencing the reality you really want to (otherwise, you wouldn't be reading this book!), and it's also worth remembering that your current reality is being created out of your current beliefs. It helps to think of your beliefs as neither right nor wrong but simply as a set of ideas about how the world works based on your current understanding and past programming. Some of the beliefs that you need to plant in order to experience the reality you desire will conflict with a few already in place; if they didn't, you'd already be living the dream. So, put aside any resistance for a few moments and don't concern yourself with whether you think a belief is true or false, but focus on the implications it would have if you believed it to be true. Then decide if you want it based on what reality it will create for you. So first of all, you need to find the specific code you use to represent things that you believe.

As we are dealing with the auditory system, you need to say something that you completely know is true and pay close attention to the way that you say it. For example, you could state your name or your date of birth. You might like to make a statement such as 'The sun will rise in the sky tomorrow' (Granted, it might be obscured by clouds, but it'll be there!) or maybe go for something simple like 'Fire is hot!' What you say doesn't matter at all; what matters is that you say something you absolutely know to be true.

Now, say something that you know isn't true, but would like it to be true, such as 'I own an Aston Martin DB9' or 'To avoid the congestion today, I flew to work in my helicopter' (If these are true… pick something else!). What you are looking for here are the differences in the submodalities of each statement. It usually helps to say a few in a row as this highlights the differences more clearly. You can also think the statements in your mind without speaking them aloud and notice any differences there too. Obviously, everyone will be different, but personally, I notice several things. My initial statements, which I completely know to be true, are said using a very 'matter of fact' tonality. They also maintain a constant pitch throughout, whereas the other statements, which I know are not true, seem to rise in pitch towards the end, almost as though I'm asking a question rather than making a statement. I also get a second internal voice after each statement. With the true statements, this is a smug little voice that says, 'Yep, it will!' (I used the sun rising option), but on the statement that I know isn't true, the secondary voice is very different; it sounds a little pissed off and a tad 'told you so', and it says, 'Don't be stupid!' The pace is slightly different too; I seem to slightly rush the false statements and sound more relaxed on the known ones.

When you do this yourself, check for other differences as well. If you are thinking the words rather than saying them aloud, remember to pay close attention to the location that the sound seems to be coming from. When you have established the submodalities used in known statements, try saying a few things that you would like to believe in this way and see how it feels. Just like the visual manipulation, you'll probably find that it sounds weird at first and things will try to revert back to their original state but be persistent; what you are doing here is training your subconscious mind to think in new ways. Even though it might take a few attempts before the subconscious gets the hang of it, once the change is accepted, it will become your new standard and the rewards will far outweigh the effort required.

While using these techniques, you're not limited to your own voice. Experiment with other voices, and see how they affect the way you feel. It really helps if you use the voice of someone who is an authority on whatever it is you are telling yourself. If you want to feel more intelligent, then pick a person that's famed for their intellect and have them tell you how intelligent you are. You might like to hear Stephen Fry or Carol Vorderman or maybe even Stephen

Hawking singing your praises and complementing you on your brilliance ('Stephen Hawking singing' is not a phrase you tend to hear very often!). If you're developing your spirituality, perhaps you'd like to invite Wayne Dyer or Deepak Chopra into your affirmations, and if you desire riches, then why not Bill Gates or Richard Branson. It can be incredibly effective to hear another person telling you how great you are, especially when they excel in whatever it is they are complimenting you on. How can you argue with the experts? If the cleverest man on Earth insists you're a genius, then how can you deny it?

As with all your meditations, spice it up and throw in all the modalities! When you see Anthony Robbins coming to tell you how much of an inspiration you have made on his life, hear his booming voice, feel his powerful handshake, and totally involve yourself in the experience. Imagine how great you'll feel when that really happens! Your subconscious mind will respond just as though it has, and the more realistic you can make it, the more amazing you'll feel. Using other people's voices is great fun, and you're only limited by your own imagination. Dare to think BIG! Imagine Gandhi telling you how compassionate you are, Einstein admiring your true genius, or Martin Luther King proudly declaring that 'YOU have a dream!' You can even experiment with fictional characters, animals, and deities. Now… it's time to really spice things up and have some fun with sounds! When you start to play with voices, you can have lots of fun and enjoy some surprising results. Try a simple affirmation, such as 'I'm totally confident and relaxed when I meet new people', and then play with the quality of the voice as you hear the affirmation in your mind. Notice how different you feel as you say the same statement with an authoritarian 'head master' tonality compared to that of a seductive temptress.

You might even like to imagine that you are these varying people as you say the statement in the 1st person, or maybe, you prefer to imagine other people saying it to you in the 3rd person. How does it affect you if you sing your affirmation? Or hear an entire choir sing it to you? What other sounds can add to the experience? Hear rapturous applause, trumpet fanfares, cheering crowds, or a complete orchestral accompaniment! Try listening to different styles of music as you read off a list of affirmations as though they were lyrics. Sing or rap them with all the panache of a superstar! There's no right or wrong way to do these exercises; just play with the suggestions and choose the ones that you find the most joyful. If you feel good, you're doing it right; it's as simple as that! While jogging, I find that running through affirmations in my head in the style of a drill sergeant and soldiers doing the Cadence 'Sound Off' chant is an amusing and powerful way of affirming motivational suggestions.

Music can be an incredibly powerful motivator, and it's a fantastic fast track method of accessing desired emotions. When Anthony Robbins set about conditioning himself to stop eating when he was full, he blasted out his favourite rock music to arouse powerful emotions, then anchored these to the action of pushing away the plate over and over again until it felt great to do it. By using carefully selected music, you can quickly and easily access powerful emotional states that can substantially improve your performance in almost any situation. While working on your manifestation meditations, being able to access specific emotions on cue is an incredibly effective tool. Obviously, different states require different triggers, so you'll need an assortment of music. If you take the time to burn a CD with a collection of songs that all inspire you in the same way, playing it while doing your manifestation meditation will massively increase your gains from the session. For example, if you want to place a cosmic order for a more financially abundant future, you might like to blast out 'We're in the money' from the musical 'Gold Diggers of 1933', and if you want to feel motivated, confident, and powerful, then Queens 'Can't stop me now' or the Rocky theme would be a great start!

When used in a way that really grabs your imagination, sound is an incredibly powerful tool for laying down new beliefs that will help you create a more desirable future, but you still need to make sure that whatever it is you're telling yourself is going to get the job done, and this is where we need to harness the awesome power of...

Positive Affirmations

Years ago, positive affirmations and auto-suggestion were hailed as the next big thing. We were all promised overnight success, and all we had to do to get it was read off a simple list of statements first thing in the morning and last thing at night. Auto-suggestion books sold like hotcakes, and millions of people leapt at the opportunity to totally transform their lives with practically no commitment or effort. It seemed too good to be true... and it was! During the auto-suggestion boon, very few people managed to achieve the success promised by the authors, and most lost faith in the process altogether. Unfortunately, many of the techniques that are incredibly powerful at transforming your life sound just like the empty promises of yesteryear. It's often all too easy to dismiss them out of hand without realising how very different the results can be with just a subtle difference in the technique. Using positive affirmations badly is easy. You grab a list of affirmations and read them out to yourself. This is what thousands of people have been doing for years. Sometimes they work but only if you're lucky enough to fluke all of the other requirements that make them effective. Usually, affirmations of this nature simply aren't powerful enough to have any effect on your subconscious mind and can even leave you in a worse position than before you started!

The problem with affirmations is two fold. Firstly, you have to make sure that you are constructing the affirmation correctly. We've already looked at some of the pitfalls of badly constructed suggestions, and how a subtle difference can totally destroy your efforts. The most important rules to follow are to keep all affirmations positive and to state them in the present tense. As long as you stick to these rules, you should be able to construct a powerful affirmation for any situation. Secondly, problems arise when you don't align your affirmations with the submodalities of ownership and certainty.

Let's take a typical affirmation that you might like to use to create a more desirable reality. For this example, we'll imagine you're single, have struggled with countless failed relationships, and want to attract someone special into your life to develop a loving friendship. Because you know that your thoughts, beliefs, and focus create your reality, you also know that saying things like 'I hate being single', 'I feel so lonely', or 'I always seem to have bad relationships' is only going to keep you trapped in the situation longer. So your first step is to create some affirmations about what you actually want rather than moaning about what you've already got. 99% of people never get this far; they remain stuck in victim consciousness blaming everyone else for their problem and bitching and moaning about it at every opportunity. When you create your affirmations, you absolutely have to state them in a positive way, so saying to yourself 'I don't want to be single any more' isn't going to work. To turn this into a positive statement, you need to switch your focus to what it is you want in its place, so now your affirmation is 'I want a loving relationship'. However, we've now broken rule number two! The affirmation focuses on wanting, not having, which can actually push that loving relationship even further away! When you create affirmations you must state them as though you already have them. Keep them in the present tense, and state ownership of your desires as though you're already enjoying them. This changes our affirmation to, 'I am in a loving relationship!' which is much more powerful.

What we have just created is similar to the kind of suggestion you might find listed in an autosuggestion book. Similar, but better! If you create your own suggestions, they will always be much more powerful than generic ones as they are much more personal to you.

Your affirmation is already well constructed, but it still needs more attention. You need to be as specific as possible. Remember, cosmic ordering is like making a telephone call. The more specific you are, the greater the chance you'll get exactly what you're looking for. You'll also recognise whatever it is you've ordered much more easily when it shows up in your life. It's usually much easier to create a list of several affirmations for each cosmic order so that you can easily cover absolutely all of the features you desire. This means your single affirmation is now growing considerably. So now, you might have a list that looks something like this...

- I am in a loving relationship
- My partner loves me dearly
- My partner and I have great fun together
- We share the same values, beliefs, and goals
- We enjoy the same hobbies and pastimes
- We have the same religious and spiritual beliefs
- I am physically attracted to my partner

Make as long a list as you desire; you might like to include personal qualities, looks, age, career, or whatever. Create your list as though you were placing an order for something that needs to actually be made and the manufacturers need you to be as specific as possible so that they can ensure the order meets all of your requirements. Now, you're armed with a very powerful list of positive, personal, and specific affirmations. Next, you need to use this list to create a blueprint for your subconscious mind, which is where manipulating submodalities comes into play. If you aren't currently in a loving relationship, your subconscious mind will already have a blueprint in place that conflicts with the new one you are trying to create. If you simply read off your list, then you're reading off a list of statements that you already know are not true and don't actually believe. So you'll naturally read them using the submodality code (or recipe) that is reserved for things that you don't expect to happen.

You need to take conscious control here and make sure you state your affirmations in the same way that you'd state a fact you absolutely know to be true. As we discovered earlier, manipulating the subtle qualities of your thoughts can change the way that you feel about them. As you begin working with positive suggestion, you may find that your old thought patterns and emotions try to creep back in, especially if the affirmations you are using represent a reality that is considerably different from the one you're currently experiencing. To get around this problem, begin by focusing on a concept rather than the specific affirmation. For example, if your affirmations are all designed to increase your personal wealth, you can simply repeat the mantra 'Wealth' to yourself while in a relaxed state. This will create associations of wealth in your mind and help you to focus on wealthy things without the resistance that could be created by using a more personal affirmation that conflicts with your currently perceived circumstances.

74

As you develop your ability to manipulate your own emotions by moving the submodalities of the affirmation, you can progress to using more personal and specific affirmations as these are much more powerful. Now, you have an incredibly powerful set of affirmations that will sink deep into your subconscious mind. Going back to the garden metaphor, what you've just created in your list is a bag of seeds that you are going to plant deep into your subconscious mind. The method you'll be using to plant the seeds—manipulating submodalities—is what enables you to get them past the groundskeeper!

This means that with a little planning and conscious effort, you can easily create a powerful new blueprint deep in your subconscious mind. This process totally transforms your belief system, which is very important because it's your beliefs that are constantly creating your reality every second of every day. Once you have conditioned yourself in such a way that your beliefs are in alignment with your desires, you'll naturally create your desired reality as though you're on autopilot. Most people don't focus on their desired outcome; instead, they focus on the lack they are experiencing and the desire for change. This is an important factor that needs to be discussed in more depth as you can easily sabotage your own success if your focus is misplaced. This brings us back to those talent show contestants that we all love to watch and explains exactly what's going on. As you already know, your reality is created from your beliefs, so you'd expect those tone-deaf contestants that truly believe they are the next big thing, to be creating a much more congruent reality. Unfortunately, a solid belief in yourself is only a part of the process; you also need to ensure your focus is correctly placed, and this is where most people fall short.

As we discovered earlier, it's important to focus on the present when working on your manifestation meditations and not dwell on the past or look to the future. When you focus on a reality that you desire, you must do it as though you were already experiencing that reality. The feelings that such a focus invokes are ones of certainty, confidence, acceptance, and knowing, and it is these feelings that attract the object of your focus into your reality. The process of getting there is the emotion of being there. These emotions are paramount to your success, and you'll learn numerous techniques to ensure your emotions are in complete alignment with the actualisation of your desires. The steps of the various manifestation meditations are like a vehicle; they supply you with the medium of transport that enables you to move into that reality. However, without the correct emotions to fuel the vehicle, it cannot take you anywhere. If you prefer to think of your manifestation process as drawing your desires to you like a magnet attracting metal, then the meditation is a huge, powerful electromagnet, and the emotion is the current that runs through it to give it power.

When your focus is misplaced, your emotions are not conducive to creating the reality you desire. Obviously, we tend to only desire those things that we don't already have, so we are immediately aware of a lack in our lives that we are trying to fill. This lack could be anything; in the case of our wannabe pop stars the lack is fame. By focusing on wanting to be a famous singer, they are not focusing on being one. This is a subtle but incredibly important difference that you absolutely have to grasp if you are to succeed with these techniques. To see for yourself how this feels, think of something that you want to achieve now; stop reading for a few minutes and focus on wanting that thing. As you do this exercise, you'll probably notice an assortment of emotions—excitement about the possibility of achieving it or anxiety or nervousness in some way. If you want it enough, you could even feel a sense of desperation. As you focus on 'wanting', you'll probably feel that this thing is in some way distant from you; you might have a sense of hopefulness and cross your fingers for good luck. You might make a wish and ask for it to be yours, maybe even saying a short prayer.

Next, take a few minutes out of reading to focus on something that you already have. Think about how it feels to have this thing, and make a new list of every emotion you experience. Your new list will be very different from your previous one. This time, you'll have things in your list, such as a sense of knowing, certainty, security, contentment, peace, and possibly a feeling of closeness to whatever it is you chose to focus on. These two sets of emotions are hugely different, and they both do very different things. The first set is created by focusing on a desire, not a possession. Each emotion in the first list acts as an instruction to the cosmos to bring you more of what you are focusing on, so you'll get exactly that—an increased sense of wanting. The only way that you can increase your sense of wanting for something is to push whatever it is you desire further away or change your current situation so that you need that thing even more. For example, if you focus on wanting more money, you'll manifest the reality of wanting it more, and the easiest and quickest way to do this is to actually have less money. When you can't pay your bills or put food on your table, the 'wanting' that you have been focusing on grows very quickly!

What you have effectively done is create a perfect reality based on your beliefs and focus. Unfortunately, your focus was incorrectly placed, so the reality you created wasn't exactly what you wanted, but it was exactly what you focused on. This hurdle is the one that trips up almost everyone that doesn't succeed using these techniques, and it comes about because of a lack of understanding about the difference between focusing on wanting something and focusing on having it.

Many people don't even realise that they are focused on wanting something rather than having it, and they'll completely insist they are doing the exercises properly; then you'll hear them state that they really want something or comment on how nice it would be to have this or that! This is focusing on wanting! When you focus on having something, you never comment on how nice it 'would' be, but how nice it 'is'.

When you use your second list of emotions, the instructions that you send out into the cosmos are congruent with your desire. They resonate at exactly the same vibration as the thing you are manifesting, and as a result, you end up with much more of it coming into your life! As you get more, it becomes easier to focus on what you have achieved, and this focus continues to attract more of the same until you shift your focus to something else. That's why the rich get richer and the poor get poorer! Of course, if you're already poor and you want to become rich, you just have to use these techniques to trick your subconscious mind into believing you're rich to get things started.

The next bit's important... so read it nice and slowly!

It's focussing on already having what you desire that creates the necessary emotions to fuel the process of manifestation. This aligns your spiritual vibration with the desire causing it to manifest into your physical reality.

And just once more for good measure (and because that was a bit of a mouthful), here's the simplified version: The process of getting whatever you desire is the emotion of already having it.

78

This is important. So if you're only half here with me and half mentally planning what's for lunch, give me your undivided attention for a few moments, jump back a paragraph or two, and read that bit again. Just to make sure it completely sinks in. And if you're like me and rarely jump back when someone asks you to, here it is once more!

The process of getting whatever you desire is the emotion of already having it.

This is the most important sentence in the entire book, so here it is again just to make absolutely sure it sinks in! The process of getting whatever you desire is the emotion of already having it.

Of course as you know, repetition is one of the ways that new ideas slip past the guardian that protects your subconscious mind allowing them take root as new beliefs. So once more won't hurt... The process of getting whatever you desire is the emotion of already having it. ...Okay that's enough!

Consciously creating any reality you desire is easy; you simply need to follow a series of steps. However, it does require discipline. Your subconscious mind has been conditioned to think a certain way for your entire life, and now, you need to condition it to think the way that you want it to think. Thoughts happen in an instant, so it's very hard to think positively all of the time because you don't know what you're going to think until you're already thinking it and by then it's too late. It's simply not possible to decide what you're going to think before it happens, so it's almost impossible to only allow yourself to have positive thoughts. The trick isn't to try to take control of your thoughts and only allow the positive ones, but to condition your thoughts so that you are more likely to think positive ones in the first place. With a little commitment in the early stages, it is surprisingly easy to…

Eliminate Negative Thinking

Negative thoughts that you notice yourself having can be incredibly useful as they expose the hidden beliefs that are holding you back, and it's these beliefs that support the reality that you are trying to move away from, so becoming aware of them will help you to do something about them. However, by conditioning your thoughts so that you stay positively focused at all times, you are ensuring that the reality you are constantly creating unconsciously is a reality that you desire.

To do this effectively, you need to become aware of your thoughts, and this is not such an easy task. We are usually so involved in the thought process that we simply don't see it happening. In order to bring your thoughts into your conscious awareness, you're going to need to step back and look at them more objectively, and this requires discipline. Whenever you notice a negative thought, there are certain things that you need to do (we'll be getting to these in a few moments); however, the difficult part is consciously noticing the negative thought in the first place. Negative thoughts produce negative emotions, so they make you feel bad. Bad feelings are a sign that you've been caught up in negative thinking. Whenever you become aware of a negative thought, use what you have learned about creating positive affirmations to create an instant affirmation to cancel the negativity out and get you back on track.

This process is incredibly effective as it enables you to constantly monitor your creative process. These affirmations will be very specific to your requirements as they address your actual situation. When most people start designing a list of personal affirmations, they rarely know which affirmations are going to be the most effective. By using this simple process of creating instant affirmations in response to negative thoughts, you are designing perfect affirmations that are best suited to your specific requirements. You are also conditioning yourself to think in a more positive way. When your thoughts are positively focused, you naturally create a positive, abundant reality.

Think back to the garden analogy. A negative belief is a seed, the resulting undesired reality is the plant that grew from that seed, and any negative thoughts that you might have as a result of that reality are the fruits of the plant. The fruit contains more seeds, and if you don't stop them, they'll grow into new plants.

This is what happens in your life when you allow your negative thoughts to go unchecked. First of all, a negative belief is planted in your mind. This develops over time and manifests in your life as a negative situation. The negative situation causes you to have further negative thoughts sowing more negative beliefs. As you can imagine, if you allow this process to continue, it can very quickly get out of control. Negative thinking is like throwing a handful of seeds into your garden. So what do you do whenever you notice yourself having a negative thought? Congratulate yourself! Give yourself a mental pat on the back and a sincere 'Well done!' Why? Well, spotting a negative thought is good news! You really want to catch as many as you can. If you congratulate yourself whenever you catch one, your subconscious mind will soon start to bring more to your conscious awareness! (Don't worry about creating an anchor to negative thinking here as you only congratulate yourself when you notice the negative thought, and by this time, your thinking has already shifted. The association is created on noticing and then changing the negative thought, not on having it.)

Once you've noticed the thought and congratulated yourself on the discovery, there are lots of things that you can do with it. The simplest and most effective thing would be to use that negative thought to instantly create some positive affirmations. So, if you notice yourself worrying about not being able to pay the bills each month, you can simple create a list of affirmations that state that you can, such as:

- I always pay my bills on time
- I have lots of money left over for myself each month after paying my bills
- I enjoy paying my bills

Having a readymade affirmation that you can use the moment you notice yourself feeling or thinking negatively is really useful, and it can quickly shift your state to a much more productive and positive place.

If you notice negative thoughts about money, a great little affirmation you can use is to think about money coming into your life, smile to yourself and say 'I love it when I receive money; it makes me feel so good'. Then imagine a specific sum of money coming into your life and begin to think about how you're going to spend it. This simple technique is usually all that is needed to shift your focus to a more productive and positive state, enabling you to move to a more desired reality. However, if you notice that you're having the same negative thoughts popping up time and time again, it's safe to assume that you have a belief hidden in your subconscious mind that supports them. In this case, the belief is probably something along the lines of...

- I can't cope
- My bills are too expensive
- I don't earn enough money
- More is going out than coming in
- I'll never be able to support my family

It helps to make a list of all of the negative beliefs you can think of that might support the negative thought you had, even if you know they aren't true. Then you can create some positive affirmations for each of these. You should move onto your positive affirmations as quickly as possible. Don't spend too long focusing on the negative beliefs as you tend to move towards (and get more of) the object of your focus. It's important to create both lists in one session. Don't write down all the negatives, then take a break as this leaves you focused on the negative list. Your new list of positive affirmations might look something like this:

- I am in control of my finances
- My bills are very reasonable
- I appreciate the resources I use and happily pay for them each month
- I earn more than enough money to pay my bills, support my family, and enjoy my life
- I dictate my earnings, and can easily increase my own wealth whenever I desire

Once you have a list of affirmations, you can simply use these during your manifestation meditation. Remember to state your affirmations in such a way—by manipulating the submodalities—

that your subconscious mind believes and accepts them. The list of positive affirmations that you create will be very powerful because they are so specific to your needs. By making notes of any negative thoughts you notice throughout the day, you can ensure that your affirmations cover all of the areas that need attention. This makes creating your affirmations much easier as it gives you a place to start. Another great way of working with thoughts as they happen is to immediately tag a positive affirmation right on the end. This works particularly well with sayings such as 'Money doesn't grow on trees'. Here you can simply tag on a statement that positively enforces your ability to create your own wealth through the use of positive focus and a belief in yourself, so the next time you hear yourself saying, 'Money doesn't grow on trees' follow it up with, 'That's right, it doesn't grow on trees, it grows out of my positive focus, my unwavering belief in prosperity, and my abundant thoughts! In other words, it grows out of me!!' This will very quickly neutralise the negative thought and provide a much more positive focus.

build affirmation list.

As you begin working with your affirmation list, you'll very quickly find that every time you hear a negative suggestion (your own or someone else's), you'll automatically create a positive affirmation to counter it. For example, if you catch yourself saying 'I'm too fat to wear this; I look ridiculous', you'll notice that almost before you finish the sentence, a second, more confident voice will hit back with a positive 'I'm gorgeous! I look fantastic in everything I wear, and I have a stunning figure!' When this begins to happen, stop writing down the negative thoughts that you notice, and simply write down the automatic affirmation that countered it. When you later set out to create your list of affirmations, simply use that one as inspiration for a few more of a similar nature. This method allows you to put as little focus into the negative belief as possible and begin focusing on a more positive alternative immediately. You might even find that you never need to write out anything negative at all. It takes only seconds to transform a negative statement into a positive affirmation.

Whether you write down the original negative thought and create your list from that or write down a counter affirmation to inspire others, you'll end up with the same list of affirmations, but focusing on the positive counter from the start will elicit change more rapidly. So far, we've looked at a couple of great ways a negative thought can be turned into positive affirmations, but what happens to the negative thought? What do we do with the negative belief that we've uncovered? By creating a set of positive affirmations that conflict with the original negative thought, we are already weakening its power over us. However, it's best to go that extra mile and completely remove the negative belief so that it never stifles your creative abundance again. There are lots of ways you can do this, so simply choose the one that you find the most joyful.

By dressing up a disempowering belief in the submodalities that you usually use for something that you don't believe, you can trick your subconscious mind into thinking that the belief isn't true. You do this exactly the same way as before; however, you really don't want to focus on the process too much as the more you focus on a belief, the more likely you are to attract it into your life. Ideally, you want to remove the belief as quickly as possible and immediately begin focusing on the more positive alternative. If you are particularly visual, then you might like to imagine the belief written out on a blackboard. Simply take the board eraser, and rub it out. Another popular method is to see the belief written in the wet sand on a beach and watch as the ocean gently washes the message away.

By using your imagination in this way, you can remove the negative belief in a lot of different ways. These techniques are a form of communication with your subconscious mind. You cannot usually communicate your desires so easily to your subconscious, but by using images in this way, you can program your mind to take the necessary action required to remove the belief without needing to understand the actual process. Any imagined representation will suffice. If you can easily relate to the garden analogy, then imagine the negative belief as a weed, and see it wither away and die. Or perhaps, you like the idea of tying your belief to a helium filled balloon and watching it float away.

When I began working with my belief system, I'd imagine dropping my negative beliefs into a bottomless well. I'd imagine them as floating text, like a cartoon speech bubble; then with a cheeky smile and a wave, I'd say 'Bye!' as I watched the belief suddenly plummet into the darkness until it vanished. When I discovered the chalk board technique, I found it much easier to visualise so switched over to that one. The process itself really isn't important. Just choose whichever technique you prefer or make up your own!

Use this

Before I developed my visualisation skills, I used to imagine that the negative belief was recorded onto a vinyl record. I'd then imagine how it would sound if I scratched the record so it couldn't play the belief properly. The needle would jump on the scratched record and suddenly skip to a positive alternative. I'd then imagine the scratch causing that positive affirmation to play over and over until it became almost hypnotic. Your subconscious mind responds incredibly well to your imagination, and you can use simple visualisations, such as shrinking a visual representation of something you no longer want to experience, to easily program your mind to change your reality.

Another powerful technique is to imagine yourself physically removing the negative belief, which really helps to detach you from the subtle energies of an experience on many levels. This method works well if the negative belief is related to another person or object. Simply become aware of a connection that binds you to the object or person and visualise it as a channel of energy. Notice the way that energy seems to be flowing through this channel as though the other person or object were in some way stealing it from you. On a subtle level, this is what is actually happening. To stop the theft, imagine grabbing hold of the channel itself and disconnecting it from your body. As you break the connection, notice the channel wither and die as it retreats back to the other person or object. Next, visualise the area of your being from which you disconnected the channel. You'll probably become aware of a hole or wound that was made as the channel was removed. To heal this, simply imagine it closing up and repairing itself. This simple meditation can be performed in a few seconds, yet it is a tremendously powerful way of breaking down energy drains that may have been with you for many years. If you were ever bullied as a child, then use this technique to disconnect yourself from the bully. Even after many years, there will often still be an energy drain going on at some level.

I was never really bullied when I was in school, but I did have some issues with a couple of people that I felt would benefit from this technique. So I recently did a quick meditation while focussing on one person in particular to remove any connection we might still have. I don't think it was ever this person's intention to do so, but some of his actions made me feel intimidated at school, and it felt as though I'd carried those feelings with me into adulthood, and they were in some way stopping me from living my true potential. I did the meditation at night just prior to sleeping. When I imagined the connection between us, it was very strong, and I could easily feel the energy being drained from my being even after 20 years. I took hold of the channel and uncoupled it from my body as one might disconnect a gas pipe. I was aware that it left a 'wound', so I imagined this closing up and healing over before I dropped off to sleep.

The next morning, I felt somewhat lighter, as though a weight had finally been lifted off my shoulders; the difference was quite noticeable. I wouldn't really say that I was ever bullied by this person; in fact, I would be surprised if he had any idea he'd intimidated me at all!

When I logged into my computer that morning, I was totally blown away to see that I had an email from this person. We hadn't spoken in almost 20 years. We were never really close friends as such, and he'd never contacted me before. When you use this technique, you're not simply working with your own issues, you are actually affecting that other person too. and as you remove the channel that connects you, you both benefit from the healing. In my case, the other person would have been aware (even if only at a subconscious level) of the way their actions had affected me and been burdened by a sense of guilt for all those years. When I disconnected the channel, I released us both from the experience, and we both benefited from the results.

Because this technique works so well for both parties, it's a really good idea to think of all the people that you might have wronged in the past, and do the meditation for them. This will not only help those people to move on from the experience, but also release you.

There are lots of books that are entirely devoted to the subject of removing negative beliefs, so this is an area that could easily fill this book many times over. Most techniques simply force you to question the belief and then explore alternatives. It's always worth bearing in mind that you have the beliefs you have now only because of past programming. We tend to form many of our beliefs during childhood and carry them with us throughout our lives without questioning their validity. When we have children of our own, we often pass on those beliefs with the very best of intentions, and over many generations, the process continues. Obviously, you believe your own beliefs; if you didn't, you simply wouldn't have them. But you are also aware that other people believe things that conflict with what you have accepted as true. This conflict of beliefs is perhaps most explicit in religion. Most people that have a strong belief in something do so exclusively, so they dismiss anything that conflicts with or challenges their representation of reality. But can they all be right?

If you consider that we create our own reality based on our beliefs, then it's obvious that everyone is experiencing a reality that confirms whatever it is they believe. In other words, their own experience acts as supporting evidence for their beliefs. This makes it very difficult for people to let go of their beliefs because in their own world they are all right. However, if a person changes their belief, very soon their reality changes too. Some people are holding onto beliefs that are keeping them trapped in a reality they despise; others have adopted a set of beliefs that enable them to live a life of joyful abundance. It helps to think of beliefs as ideas. As we know, beliefs do change; we constantly discover new things that discredit previous thinking, and there are many things that simply can't be explained by the laws that we have already accepted as truth. Whatever you believe right now is creating your experience of reality.

When you notice a belief that might be holding you back or you have a thought that you might consider negative, ask yourself this question: 'Is there another belief I could adopt that would serve me better?' If there is, use the techniques in this book to swap those beliefs. You'll discover a great way to do this later when we explore the NLP swish pattern. When you think thoughts, you send out energy, and that energy can be measured by its vibration. If you think negative thoughts, the energy that you send out into the cosmos has a slow vibration; if you think positive thoughts, the frequency of the vibration is much faster and higher. As your thoughts reach out into the cosmos, they attract things to you that are vibrating at the same frequency. If you thoughts are negative, the things you attract will be negative too.

Aside of your life experiences, objects, events, situations, and emotions, your thoughts attract something else too... and they do this incredibly well. They attract other people that are broadcasting similar thoughts! You'll often find that a group of close friends are transmitting thoughts of a very similar frequency. As they are all transmitting similar thoughts, they all attract similar experiences. So it's very easy for them to compare stories that back up each others' beliefs because they are essentially creating very similar realities. As you begin to work on your beliefs and consciously raise the quality of your thoughts, you'll find yourself out of sync with your usual circle of friends. When this happens, it's not uncommon for your entire circle of friends to very suddenly change. You'll find yourself meeting new people that are sending out thoughts of the same vibration that you are now sending and you'll seem to drift away from old friends because you are very literally 'no longer on the same wavelength'.

As your vibration begins to shift outside that of your circle of friends, a few things might happen. You might find that you inspire them to follow, and you all move to a new place together. You could find that they object to your shift and try to bring you back to their level by offering you validation of your previous beliefs. You might notice that they begrudge the progress you've made as it exposes their own failings. Some people will do anything they can to sabotage your success just to make themselves feel better about their own situation.

For these reasons, I'd strongly suggest that you simply don't tell people you are using these techniques at least until you have some really solid evidence that it's working for you. To begin with, keep your meditations private and only talk about what you are doing with those that you know will be encouraging and positive. We've already talked about conditioning your own beliefs, but it's also important to consider the beliefs of others and how they affect your life. Remember my oak tree? The seed represents the original belief, the tree represents the reality that belief creates, and the acorns on the tree represent the thoughts I have because of that reality. What happens if I take an acorn from the tree and throw it into my neighbour's garden? Well, if my neighbour doesn't remove the acorn, eventually the seed will take root and grow into a new oak tree, in his garden!

When your well-meaning friends try to protect you from 'all that new age mumbo jumbo crap', they are throwing their seeds into your garden! If you allow them to take root, they'll grow! And before you know it, you'll have adopted their beliefs and begin experiencing their version of reality.

This is how it works in real life…

You stumble across a book that teaches you how to create anything you want, like this one! You're obviously excited and eager to get started, so you follow the instructions and begin to condition your thoughts. Your discipline pays off! You quickly begin sending out higher frequency vibrations. Your raised energy transmissions act like magnets and start to draw the objects of your desires to you. Although you can't see it yet, everything you've ever wanted turns its attention your way and embarks on a journey through space and time into your reality. However, just before it reaches you, you decide that your friends could really use a technique like this, so you tell them what you've been up to... Big mistake!

Your friends have already subconsciously noticed you're changing, and they're threatened! They're about to lose a close buddy, get a stark reminder of how little they're doing to change their own situation, and have one less person to moan to about how crap life is! This is not good news! They need you back where you were: life was simple, life was easy, life was comfortable... OK... it was crap, but at least when yours was crap too, they felt better about theirs! So... What do they do? They throw a bunch of dirty seeds all over your garden! They bombard you with negative suggestions all neatly wrapped up in reasons why you're being fooled and everything you've just told them is rubbish. They'll have some really convincing arguments too, as their experience causes them to firmly believe that what you're doing isn't going to work!

Their argument will sound convincing to the unprotected, as they're drawing on a reality that you very recently shared. The seeds will begin to take root; beliefs will begin to form. Before you know it, you'll have allowed those seeds of suggestion to grow, and like a weed strangling a precious flower, doubt will begin to smother your dreams. The solution? Don't tell them! ...and if you absolutely have to tell them, protect yourself first! Not telling your friends what you're up to is the obvious solution. You really should keep these techniques to yourself until you have an unwavering belief in your ability and lots of physical proof that can withstand the onslaught of 'It's all coincidence... don't be so naïve!'

When you're bullet proof, shout about it! Tell everyone what you've accomplished and how! However... until then, mums the word! Protecting yourself from other people's negativity is also extremely important in the early stages as every negative comment you are subjected to can sneak its way into your experience if you're not on your toes. Just as there are lots of ways to extinguish your own negative thoughts, there are also lots of ways to protect yourself from other people's negative thoughts. It all comes down to your imagination. Remember: if you can imagine it, you can program your subconscious mind to create it! So, let's create some protection!

I remember, a few years ago, I was listening to a seminar by Dr. Wayne Dyer. He talked about an experience he'd had on a plane that really stuck with me. The plane had been delayed and additional complications had caused more than a little annoyance in the rest of the passengers, and as each passenger boarded the plane, they targeted the stewardess who was welcoming them aboard. Obviously, the delay wasn't her fault, but she was the face of the company, so she bore the brunt of their frustration. Each person passing either had something nasty to say about the airline or complained about the delay. As she absorbed all the negative comments, they began to grind her down, and as you would expect, her mood soon reflected the abuse. When Wayne boarded the plane, he noticed her depleted state and offered a simple solution that I think we can all benefit from: he told her about the layers of protection that she had to shield herself from the barrage of negative comments. She'd taken the comments far too personally, yet they weren't really meant for her; they were meant for the company she represented. Unfortunately, the negative comments were being channelled through her, and her first line of defence was the thing that she used to associate herself with the company: her uniform!

Wayne taught her how to use her name badge and uniform to protect herself from the negative comments so that she wouldn't have to absorb them. He simply suggested that she see the uniform as a force field that stopped any negative energy getting through to her. As the plane landed, she imagined her protective shield and allowed her uniform to absorb the comments as the passengers left. She simply stood behind her imaginary barrier and smiled politely at each passenger.

Aside of a uniform, we all carry several layers of protection that with a little imagination, we can turn into a force field that absorbs or repels negative comments from others. Our clothes work great, as does our skin. You can even imagine that your body itself is a layer of protection. You're not your body; it's simply a vehicle that you require to experience this physical reality. When I was studying with the National Federation of Spiritual Healers (NFSH), we often used a protective meditation to close down our Chakra centres and keep us shielded from negative energy. This was called the protective egg breath (I always thought this was a very bizarre choice). The name wasn't derived from smelly breath, but the egg shape of the human aura that surrounds the body and of course breathing!

The meditation was very simple; to do it, you imagine an egg shape around your body that changes colour as your breathe. The colours are those of the visual spectrum. So you start with red and then move progressively through orange, yellow, green, blue,

95

indigo, violet and finally white. To start with, you visualise your egg as bright red and focus on the 'egg shell' above your head. As you breathe in, shift your focus down one side of the egg until, at the end of your in-breath, your focus is directly beneath you. Then, you simply move up the other side as you breathe out. After this, you do a second, similar breath while focusing on moving around the egg by going straight down the back and up the front. Once you're back at the top, you move on to the next colour and do it all again.

Protecting yourself with oddly named meditations isn't something I personally recommend, simply because I don't do it nor have I ever felt the need to do it. I've always felt perfectly safe in my own body, and negative energy very rarely crosses my mind. I've met many incredibly spiritual people that never 'close down their chakras' or use any form of self protection what-so-ever, but I've also met people that are totally horrified by the thought of 'leaving yourself so exposed'.

I can't tell you what you should do yourself, but I can tell you what I do, and maybe, that will work for you too. Remember, your imagination is incredibly powerful; when you imagine something, you create it. When you imagine an egg shaped force field around your body, you create one, and if you believe, it'll protect you against any negative energy, it will!

Although I just told you that I don't protect myself, I actually do but I didn't realise that's what it was. I just do what I do because it's fun and it feels good! I use two very simple techniques to 'protect' myself from negativity although the first is my favourite. This is to simply imagine I am made of pure light! It's very pleasant to meditate on the idea of being made of light, and it's actually much closer to the truth of our nature of existence than many people realise. When I'm visualising myself as light, I glow (not literally of course; just in my imagination!). As I glow, light comes out of me and shines on everything and everyone I touch. To me, this light is incredibly powerful positive energy that helps to raise the spiritual vibration of whatever is in its glow.

I like to play with this light energy and often blast some at people (or situations) that I think might need it. This is great fun to do as you're walking through town. Until very recently, I lived in a town centre, so I'd walk through town a lot. As I'd happily wander through the streets, I'd imagine myself as a pure body of light and often blast a passer-by with some of that light to help them feel a little more positive or boost their health. I tend to blast people that look depressed, bored, lonely, or ill.

The 'blast' is a bit like sending out bolts of lightning. Every now and then, the person I just blasted suddenly looks up at me, and every once in a while, someone flashes me a 'thank you' smile that really makes me feel great! Blasting people with this light energy isn't restricted to those people I can see; I often send it out to people in other countries and even other times, such as people (myself included) that had an impact on my childhood.

This glowing light works as protection because I always imagine any negative energy that's sent my way as a shadow, and as you know, if you shine a light at a shadow, it instantly disappears. I find this is more than enough to protect myself, and it's great fun. It's also one of those things you can do whenever and wherever you like—you don't need to sit in a special position or close your eyes. It works very well for me, so if you feel, you need a little protection try it yourself.

The second thing I do has changed over the years. Originally, I would imagine I had a mirror-like force field all over my body like a second skin that reflected all negative energy back to the person that sent it. This worked great for me, but not so great for the other person, so I tweaked it a little. While undergoing my initiation ceremony to become a magnified healer, I was introduced to the ascended master beloved lady Quan Yin. One of the reasons she is with us is to transmute negative energy using a sacred violet fire. As part of the healing work that I do, I have to send energy up to her violet fire for transmutation. That energy becomes positive energy and is distributed as required. This makes sense to me as energy doesn't die; it simply changes form. So I like the idea of taking something negative, transforming it into something positive and then sending it back to its origin. This seemed like a much better way to 'protect myself', so I applied it to my 'mirror'. My new mirror has violet flames rolling through it, and whenever any negative energy is sent my way, it is transformed into positive energy before being sent back.

All of this works and exists only because I imagine it. I could, if I wanted to, imagine an egg around my body instead or a series of colours. I could wear a trinket and invest my belief in that or carry a lucky charm; you should do whatever you feel is right for you. The people that you associate with will often say things that are detrimental to your progress, but remember that everything they say doesn't have to be your truth; it is their truth. If they believe it, they will create it as their reality. As soon as you recognise and accept that we all create our own reality, you can accept that it's OK for others to express their negative views about what you are doing without allowing them to stifle your growth.

In the opening chapter to this book, I told you about the house we created. The day we moved was totally perfect in every way. I also told you about our friends that were moving but were certain something would go wrong. They constantly bombarded us with negative comments. If we'd allowed their negativity to poison our own thoughts, something would have gone wrong. Their belief created that very reality for themselves when their buyer pulled out at the last minute. Focusing on anything negative is what draws it to you. If you are going to be subjected to a barrage of negative comments from work colleagues, family, or friends, then you should make sure you protect yourself first. In your normal day to day experience, you'll be subjected to all kinds of negativity without even realising it. By far the biggest culprit of this is the TV! I own a TV, I watch it regularly, but I'm very selective about the programs I watch. Aside of catching the odd one or two while at friends' homes, I haven't seen a news broadcast in about 8 years. I also never ever read newspapers. I don't feel in any way out of touch with reality. I still know what's going on in the world because it's pretty much all everyone talks about. But I've removed myself from the onslaught of negative media coverage that does noting more than distribute negative energy.

There are practically unlimited positive stories that could be reported, and any one of these would leave us all feeling great, but unfortunately, it's the negative stuff that our media world tends to focus on.

This can be a serious problem because you create the object of your focus! If you watch a news broadcast about a poor old lady being mugged in the street, then you'll naturally start to think about it. Before the broadcast, your thoughts were elsewhere, and you were investing no energy whatsoever into creating such a reality, but as you watch the story unfold on the screen, a seed is planted in your mind that begins to spew out negative thoughts one after the other. You probably won't even consciously notice it happening, but thoughts such as 'It's not safe on the streets', 'What's the world coming to', 'People have no morals these days', etc. etc. will suddenly be flooding your mind. Thoughts without emotion are not very powerful, so not every thought you have is going to create its own reality. However, if you get caught up in these thoughts and begin to worry, you're suddenly a reality creating powerhouse!

This problem exacerbates when literally millions of people are all having the same thoughts at the same time! This happens a lot when we experience global disasters or war. Fortunately, whenever there's a global catastrophe, people seem to put aside their differences and help one another. We suddenly become much more caring, and everyone does their very best to support those in need. Nothing brings out community spirit better than a disaster. Did you notice what just happened?

Within the space of a couple of paragraphs, you shifted from a state of worrying because of an old lady being mugged to feeling warm emotions of wholesome community spirit, simply because I suggested it. This happens constantly, so it's really important to focus on the positive stories, and not allow yourself to get caught up in negative thinking because of someone else's misfortune. The best and easiest way to do this by far is to not subject yourself to the negative story in the first place. Switch off the TV! It's as simple as that. If you do hear a negative news story—whatever it's about—think about a positive alternative. I totally guarantee that the positive situation is happening to someone in the world; the media just don't bring those things to your attention. The next time you hear of an old lady being mugged, make up your own news story about a young lad helping to bring joy back to some lovely dear old ladies at the local old folks home by playing some classic wartime favourites on the piano while everyone sings along! Roll out the barrel... we'll have a barrel of fun!! Knees up mother brown... Knees up mother brown!! See how much better you suddenly feel? Easy isn't it!

Everything in life has a natural cycle. We all have our ups and downs. Even when you have successfully conditioned yourself to be incredibly positive and optimistic, you'll still be aware of a certain ebb and flow to the process. Sometimes, you will naturally feel more positive than at other times. This is just the way nature works. If you notice yourself feeling negative about a situation, you need to change your state as quickly as possible. Negative emotions are a signal from your higher (and more knowledgeable) self that whatever you are focusing on is taking you away from whatever you desire! This is the great thing about negative emotions. If you notice one—it doesn't matter what it is, just think of it as an alarm. Every single negative emotion you have is an alarm telling you that your current thinking is working against you. For example, let's pretend that you have reason to believe that your partner is cheating on you; this thought makes you feel jealous, which is a negative emotion. Emotions (good and bad ones) fuel manifestation of focus, so if you focus on your partner cheating, and you feel a strong emotion as you do (i.e. jealousy), then this is going to draw that experience to you. To avoid this process, you need to recognise that every negative emotion you experience is your higher self warning you that your current thoughts are creating a reality that do not want. Negative emotions are your inner alarm screaming at you to stop focusing on whatever it is that makes you feel the emotion. Usually, you need only recognise what thoughts cause the negative response and think the exact opposite to elicit a more favourable positive emotion that will lead to a state you do desire. For example, if you notice you are worried (negative emotion!) that you can't pay your bills, then that will be your experience. Your focus is on not paying bills, and the fuel that brings that experience to you is worry. As soon as you recognise a negative emotion, you should immediately identify what thought caused it. In this case, the original thought would have been something like 'I won't be able to pay my bills!' To turn this around, you simply create the affirmation 'I always pay my bills easily' and create a positive emotion to draw that experience to you. When you already feel negative, it can seem difficult to break yourself out of a downward spiral—negative thoughts lead to negative experiences and these create more negative thoughts! To make the shift to a more positive state, you need to do something that makes you feel good, and it must be easy to do, as the very time that you need to do it is the exact time that you'll least want to do anything! You need to...

Feel More Positive!

Feeling positive is great! It helps you to focus on what you want much more easily, and it enables you to get it fast! When you focus on your desires, having positive emotions about them is one of the quickest ways to make sure they manifest into your life. Let's do a little experiment (You're going to have to get up for this one, so I hope you're alone! If you're not, then make sure you come back and do this later; it's surprisingly powerful!).

We're going to do a little acting. To start off, I want you to act as though you were really confident—get up and stride around the room just as you would if you were feeling 100% confident. Notice your body posture and experiment a little to see if you can really boost that feeling of confidence. You'll probably find that standing up tall, with your shoulders back and your head held high helps. It also really helps to imagine a cloak draped around your shoulders and dragging on the floor behind you as you confidently stride around the room. Notice how your actual confidence builds just because you are moving in a confident way and adopting a confident posture.

Next, we'll experiment with a negative emotion. This time we're going to act depressed. You can sit for this one if you prefer or slowly saunter around the room with a slumped posture and your head lolling forward. We don't want to practise feeling depressed for too long. Just act depressed for long enough to notice how your actual state changes from the confidence you were feeling a few moments ago.

That's enough of that... let's get back to the positive shall we? This time I want you to act as though you were excited! Really pull out all the stops! Don't act like an excited adult; adults are terrible at expressing excitement. We tend to think it's embarrassing to really show how we feel, so we stifle our emotions and rarely let our feelings truly flow. For this exercise, imagine you are a child again and today is your birthday!

Remember to use all of your acting ability to really step into your new role. Jump up and down just as an excited young child might, open your eyes wide, gasp at the enormous pile of presents in front of you, and feel a huge grin spreading across your face as the rush of excitement floods your entire body. As soon as you feel totally excited (if you don't yet, then get up and jump around some more!!), it's time to discover something kind of strange and very useful. While acting as excited as you possibly can, with your eyes wide open, a huge grin across your face, and a 'Woohoooo!!' bursting to escape from your mouth, I want you to try to feel depressed. Don't stop acting excited at all. Keep the same excited posture, the same movement and expression, but at the same time, try to feel depressed. Difficult isn't it! If you're not alone, get up and dash off to the loo! Lock the door and do this! It's really powerful stuff and way too much fun to skip!

Throughout this book, we explore various ways to manifest our desires by deliberately accessing the emotions that those desires would naturally cause us to experience, and the exact same thing is happening here! We are using the physical posture that an emotion would naturally elicit to create the emotion. The wonderful thing is that when we adopt the posture of a positive emotion, it's very difficult for us to feel a negative one at the same time, so if you are trapped in a negative cycle and you need to quickly and easily break free, all you have to do is get up and jump around like a child! What could be simpler than that? It's child's play... literally! And... as always, the more fun you have doing it, the more powerful that emotional shift will be.

If you find yourself trapped in the darkest pits of depression, it might seem like a long way to excitement, but it only takes a very small step to get started, and after that, it's easy! Just get up, have a walk around, and shake yourself about. That's all it takes to break you out of a negative state. Whenever I feel as though I have slipped into a negative state, I like to imagine that the actual emotion itself is a very thin layer of fragile plaster that has set around my body. I recognise that I attracted the 'negative plaster' to my being by focusing on negative thoughts, and it managed to set because my posture was negative too. The moment I break that posture by walking around and having a good shake the fragile layer shatters into a thousand pieces and falls away from me. I then dust myself off and adopt the posture and thoughts of a positive emotion that I'd prefer to feel and consciously invite this into my experience. I visualise the positive emotion as a flexible light body or cloak that wraps all around me and soaks deep into every cell, molecule, and electron of my body.

This technique is primarily used to make you feel good when you're feeling bad, but it's much more versatile than that. Different positive emotions can be accessed by adopting different positions. Sometimes, simply 'feeling good' isn't specific enough for your needs; you might want to feel confident, but not excited. To do this, simply act confident. Confident people hold their head high, make confident gestures as they speak, have a powerful handshake and a walk that says 'I'm important!' Whatever emotion you wish to experience can be activated by first adopting the posture you would have if you were already feeling that emotion. Once you've made the initial shift, the new emotion you'll have triggered will enhance the posture, which in turn will increase the emotional state.

Being able to alter your state when you feel bad is a very useful and powerful tool. Feeling bad is your higher self communicating to you that your thoughts are not in alignment with your desires, so shifting yourself into a more positive state is very important. By creating a powerful association between a desired state and trigger, you can access that state whenever you need it incredibly quickly. This process is called...

Anchoring

Anchoring is a fantastic tool for accessing emotions on cue, which makes it really handy for cosmic ordering. Ideally, you should set up various anchors so you have quick access to different states as you need them. To create an anchor, you need two things: the state (or emotion) that you wish to harness and a trigger that you will use to access the state. An anchor works because of association; therefore, to create an anchor, you need to create an association between the state and the trigger. Once your mind has connected the two, you'll find that you can easily access the state whenever you need to by simply firing off the trigger. The first anchoring experiment, and by far the most famous, was Pavlov's dog. During this experiment, Ivan Pavlov, a Russian physiologist, psychologist, and physician, successfully trained many dogs to salivate at the sound of a bell. He achieved this very simply by ringing the bell at the same time as offering the dogs food, and after a while, the dogs naturally created an association that connected the ringing sound to food, eliciting salivation, the response to the presence of food. Before long, the ringing bell was all that was required to induce salivation.

This discovery, as simple as it sounds, is incredibly important, and many NLP strategies that have only very recently been developed use this principle to elicit massive change in seconds that can completely transform a person's life. Anchors actually happen all of the time and can often be the cause of an irrational fear or phobia. Most people have lots of very pleasant anchors that are triggered by music. When you are experiencing a strong emotion, your subconscious mind will link this feeling to your perception at the time. The link could be made to anything in your experience; it may be attached to a sound, an image, a sensation, a smell, or a taste. For example, when I was young, I really enjoyed tinned fruit, and one day, after arriving home from the hospital, I was treated to my favourite dessert to help me feel better. I'd needed an operation because of an accident, and the anaesthetic had made me feel really ill. As I ate the fruit, the illness exacerbated, and I was violently sick. Since that day, the taste, smell, and even sight of tinned fruit makes me feel ill.

More recently, I unintentionally created a rather unusual anchor...

Being English, I drink lots of tea, and being somewhat lazy (or organised depending on which way you look at it), if I get up to do something, I often try to do a few things at once. So if I need to go to the toilet, I pop the kettle on on the way so that it is boiled, ready to make tea when I get back. I did this a few times without giving it much thought, and the next thing I knew, I'd created an anchor. The trigger: filling the kettle; the state: needing a wee! This association became so strong that even if I'd just emptied my bladder and definitely didn't need to go, the moment I began filling the kettle, I would instantly be desperate for the loo.

I could collapse this anchor, as it's totally impractical, but I've left it in place, as every time it happens, it reminds me how powerful anchors are and encourages me to create more of them.

This is really handy as I tend to drink a lot of tea, so I get several reminders throughout the day.

Obviously, you'll be creating much more practical anchors that you can use during your meditations to create states that'll help you to manifest your desired reality quicker. Perhaps, the most useful anchor to set up at this stage is one that puts you in the mood to do the meditations in the first place. When I began writing this book, progress was incredibly slow as there were far too many things that I enjoyed doing more, such as watching TV or playing on my computer. I knew that if I was ever to get it finished, I'd need to spend much more time on it, but I also knew that I only write well when I'm in the mood. So I created an anchor that enabled me to access that mood quickly and easily. Now, whenever I have a few spare minutes, I fire off the trigger for that anchor a couple of times before I decide whether I'm going to lounge in front of the TV, buy things I don't need from ebay, or come here to talk to you. Before using the anchor, I usually just feel like watching TV, but after I've fired it off a few times, I almost always reach for the laptop and really enjoy working on the book.

This method works really well because it not only enables me to spend more time writing, it also makes me want to write and enjoy doing it! If I weren't enjoying writing this book, I definitely wouldn't finish it, and it'd be a much less enjoyable read. Creating a similar anchor will really help you to discipline yourself to do your manifestation meditations regularly and enjoy doing them. When you enjoy the process and have fun, the meditations are much more effective. To give you an idea of how creating anchors works in practise, I'll quickly run you through the anchor I created to encourage me to spend more time writing. First of all, I had to create the state I wanted to anchor. This state had to be one where I really wanted to write, so I needed lots of motivation and enthusiasm. I decided that the most motivated person I could think of was a boxer making his way into the ring to fight for a world title. I used this image to create a scene in my mind of making my way through cheering crowds with the Rocky theme booming out across the stadium. I flexed my fingers and did a little 'air-typing' for the crowd as I climbed over the ropes into the ring. My laptop was on a desk in the centre of the ring; my coach removed my robe, and I sat at the desk with my fingers poised over the keys. The air was electric as the cheering crowds fell silent, anticipating the bell. As the bell chimed, my fingers fell to the keys, and a huge beam of light immediately burst from the top of my head straight up into the sky. A wealth of spiritual wisdom and insight poured down from the heavens and flowed straight through my body as my fingers typed furiously and the words streamed effortlessly onto the screen. The crowd erupted all around me as more and more words spilled out through my fingers. Huge screens hung all around the stadium, and everyone cheered with delight as they read the book as it was born.

The scene totally seduced my senses making me want to grab my laptop and start typing more than anything I'd ever wanted before. As the desire to type peaked, I fired off my trigger, creating a strong association with the experience. My trigger was simply clenching both fists and saying 'Book!' You can use anything you want as long as it's simple enough to repeat easily when you need it. After breaking state (by jumping around a bit and having a good shake), I repeated the process a few more times to ensure that the trigger had been set, cementing the anchor in place so that I could access the desire to work on my book whenever I needed it. Now, all I need to do is fire off the trigger, and that desire to work on my book comes flooding back to me in an instant.

Anchors act like switches allowing you to turn different emotional states on as you need them. This really helps to speed things up, and it makes accessing positive states much easier, especially if you are feeling a little down. Having a technique that enables you to access a desired emotional state on cue is like filling your car with petrol when you want it to take you somewhere. The emotions are what attract the object of your focus to you. All emotions work this way; when you are focused on something at the same time as feeling an emotion, that thing will be drawn to you just as a magnet attracts metal.

The power of the attraction varies depending on the power of the emotion; strong emotions will bring things to you much more quickly—strong positive emotions bring you your desires, but strong negative ones draw those things to you that you really don't want to manifest in your life. This is why it is so important to become consciously aware of any negative emotions you experience. If you spend all day worrying about something, you are attracting that very thing to you. The good news is that positive emotions are much more powerful than negative ones, so every time you notice any negative thoughts, fire off a trigger to access a more positive state, then go through the process described previously and cancel the negative thought out with some truly empowering positive affirmations.

Positive affirmations are really just mini programs that tell your subconscious mind what you desire. They are the map that lets your mind know where you want to go, and emotion is the vehicle that will take you there. Positive affirmations can be used to transform your life in any way that you desire—you might like to increase your confidence or even boost your sexual prowess. They can also be used to attract objects into your life, such as a new car, a sum of money, or a dream home. You can even attract situations, like chance encounters, learning experiences, or a new career. They are simply statements of intent that tell your subconscious mind what you want. It then sets about doing whatever is necessary to attract that desire to you.

Getting these little programs into your subconscious mind can be a little taxing, but by manipulating the submodalities as described earlier, you can trick your subconscious mind relatively easily and enjoy fairly remarkable results. There are other ways that you can slide a message past the conscious scrutiny of your critical factor and plant it deep in your subconscious mind. Some of these are shockingly simple; others are stunningly clever, so let's now take a look at some cunning techniques you can use for...

Planting the Seeds

Anything you try to tell yourself to elicit change in your life probably conflicts with what you already believe—if it didn't, you wouldn't be wanting it! The guardian of your subconscious mind doesn't really like conflict and will resist your affirmations if they are incongruent with those you have previously accepted as truth. However, there are ways around this little problem; all you need to do is deliver your new suggestion in a way that guarantees it will be accepted.

We've already explored this area in some depth when we discussed submodalities. Remember, your mind has specific ways of thinking about things. It thinks about things you love differently to things that you do not really care for, and it has its own little pattern for processing thoughts about things you crave and a different one for things you despise. The way you process the thoughts you believe is very different to the way that you process those you don't. It's relatively simple to take advantage of this system once you have explored it enough to recognise its rules.

Dressing up a new affirmation that you want your subconscious to accept as truth in the guise of information you already believe wholeheartedly is a great way to slip in a new program past the guardian, but there are some even easier ways that you can do this immediately without practise! Perhaps the simplest of all is repetition. If you repeat an affirmation to yourself regularly, it will have an accumulative effect on your subconscious and will very quickly begin to sculpt new beliefs deep in your mind. Unfortunately, most people are already doing this with negative suggestions that keep them firmly trapped in undesirable circumstances. Perhaps, the most prolific of all is the degrading utterance 'I'm too fat!'. Repeating any negative phrase to yourself over and over is a sure-fire way to sabotage your own potential and keep you exactly where you don't want to be... or worse!

Most people simply accept the running commentary of the voice in their mind without giving much thought to its origin. We simply listen to what it has to say and accept its criticism blindly. That voice is you! In fact, all those voices are you. Some people have so many it's hard to keep track. The most I've ever encountered in a client was 14! Each had its own personality; some were encouraging and positive, but most were outrageously destructive. Whatever goes on in your head, remember one thing: You are in control of any and all voices that tell you anything. You can choose to listen to positive, uplifting, and inspiring voices that tell you how wonderful you are, or you can listen to negative babble that spends all day finding new ways to put you down.

Talking to yourself (mentally, not out loud) is one of those things you can do whenever and wherever you fancy, and no one need know what you're up to. If you make the conscious decision to only tell yourself nice things, that will make you feel good. Then you have an incredibly powerful self programming system that can lay down some very empowering affirmations. Of course, you know all this already. We've already talked about the power of affirmations at length, but now we're going to explore ways that really hammer them home and ensure that you stay focused on them for much longer... meaning you'll get whatever you desire much more quickly!

To take the effort out of repetition, just think of a tune that loops. Lots of songs and nursery rhymes do this very well. 'Three blind mice' is a great example of this, as the last line has the same tune and words as the first line, which makes it loop back on itself so you can repeat it endlessly. When you loop something in this way, after a while, the words seem to lose their conscious meaning and ease their way deep into your subconscious more easily. This rather crude method of repetition is very powerful. In fact, advertising companies spend millions of dollars creating jingles that emulate this process so they can get their sales message or brand name imprinted into your subconscious.

To start making this process work for you, just replace the lyrics of your favourite looping jingle with your positive affirmations, then let it roll! I regularly use the three blind mice tune to deliver affirmations to my subconscious. I find that this technique works best if you do it in time with your breathing or walking. This also forces you to focus inwardly which helps you to achieve a state of consciousness that is more conducive to change.

Another great way to state your affirmations is to shift the emphasis on each repetition. This not only causes numerous repetitions per affirmation, but it also changes the way that they affect you. For example, if you are using the affirmation 'I earn five thousand pounds every month', then you repeat it seven times with emphasis on each word in turn, like this:

"**I** earn five thousand pounds every month."

"I **earn** five thousand pounds every month."

"I earn **five** thousand pounds every month."

"I earn five **thousand** pounds every month."

"I earn five thousand **pounds** every month."

"I earn five thousand pounds **every** month."

"I earn five thousand pounds every **month**."

You might also like to repeat the affirmation a few times emphasising more than one word. Try it now and notice the way that doing something as simple as shifting the emphasis to a different word makes the affirmation feel more empowering. You'll very quickly be able to identify where you need to place the emphasis in order to make the affirmation feel the most realistic, and you can then use this version in a loop if you wish. Repeating affirmations doesn't have to be confined to your voice; you can also write them out. Writing out your affirmations by hand forces you to focus on them and involves more of your senses than sound alone. When you write out your affirmations, use a little imagination to enhance the process. Different coloured pens are a great start, as the colour variations help to stimulate your senses. If you really want to gain the greatest benefit from this process, then you should make a poster about your affirmations; this can be really enjoyable and incredibly powerful. Keep it light hearted and fun—you might even like to pretend you're a child again and create your own unique piece of artwork that represents your positive affirmation. Use lots of bright colours and positive symbols that compliment your affirmation. You can also cut pictures from catalogues and stick them onto the page to form a collage. As you are reading this, if you find yourself resisting such suggestions, then you are thinking with your mature conscious mind. You're looking at the exercise through the eyes of an adult and judging it based on whether you think it would be effective or not. This exercise isn't for your conscious mind; it's designed to stimulate your subconscious. Your subconscious mind still knows how it feels to be a child—it knows how to have fun and it loves bright colours and attractive images. Making a poster to celebrate your affirmation is a great way to indulge that inner child and really stimulate your subconscious mind into new ways of thinking.

Before he was a world famous hypnotist, Paul McKenna made use of a very similar technique to eliminate his debt problems. He simply 'manufactured' false bank statements by sticking different parts of his real bank statements together. He printed off a list of more desirable transactions and changed the figures on the statement to represent a healthier balance. Once he'd created his new statement, he stuck everything together and photocopied it so it looked just like the real thing. He then used this bank statement as a prop to stimulate the genuine emotional response from his subconscious mind that was needed to magnetise that reality to him. His technique obviously paid off!

Creating a metaphor to plant new beliefs in your subconscious mind is also very effective. You already have a metaphor that you can use for this; just imagine you have a magical seed that you can imbue with whatever qualities you desire, and then imagine you are planting it deep into the garden of your mind so that it grows into an empowering new belief. I often use a variation of this technique where I imagine a magical pill that I swallow in a similar way. If you take vitamin supplements each day, you can combine this creative visualisation with the physical process of taking the tablet. Just use your imagination to fill the vitamin with your desires, then swallow it and know that those qualities will very soon begin spreading throughout your body. It sounds silly but it works. The next time you take a vitamin, spend a few minutes telling yourself that it also contains incredible self confidence. Make sure you use all the tricks we've discussed so your subconscious mind accepts your suggestion. Then pop the pill and notice how incredibly confident you soon begin to feel!

As you begin to experiment, you'll probably develop your own techniques. Use these suggestions as inspiration and see what you can come up with. Getting a suggestion into your subconscious mind really helps to stimulate new beliefs and clean out the old ones. Planting new empowering suggestions and affirmations is an incredibly powerful mind conditioning exercise, and by continuing to focus on your suggestions a little each day, you are essentially feeding them, allowing them to grow into positive life changing beliefs quickly. Regular focus is the key to success here. If you cram a month's worth of focus into a day, then neglect your suggestion for the other 30, you run the risk of old beliefs and negative thoughts taking over when your new suggestions are most vulnerable. Staying focused on your desires will really help you to achieve them much more quickly. This is the basic concept behind some of the most powerful self improvement programs available. Anthony Robbins' 'hour of power' is a fine example of this in action; however, there is a much easier way to get whatever you desire.

This technique is probably the laziest way to success imaginable simply because you employ a 'tool' to do all of the work for you. You just sit back and go about your business. The purpose of the tool is to keep your subconscious mind focused on your positive affirmations. This is achieved by using subliminal programming software. Very simply, what this piece of clever software does is to periodically flash positive affirmations on your computer screen. Each time a message is flashed on the screen, your subconscious mind is conditioned towards a new and more desirable way of thinking.

Affirmations are incredibly powerful. When you tell yourself something over and over, it has a huge effect on you. You can see this for yourself very easily if you try the following experiment. You'll need the assistance of a friend for this one, but it's certainly worth doing so go grab your buddy and meet me back here when you're ready.

To start, instruct your friend to hold their arm straight out to their side at shoulder height. Your job is to push their arm down; their job is to resist you as much as possible and try to keep their arm in place. You can swap over and try it the other way around afterwards if you wish. Before you begin pressing down on their arm, give them the instruction to repeat the affirmation 'I am really weak, I am really weak' over and over out loud. While they are doing this, you might like to say the affirmation 'I am really strong, I am really strong' over and over in your head... but don't let them hear you saying it! Now push their arm down. Once their arm is down at their side (which shouldn't take very long if they are following your instructions) go back to the start position, and this time have them repeat the affirmation 'I am really strong, I am really strong', and you quietly think to yourself 'I am really weak, I am really weak.' Try again to push down their arm and notice the difference. If you want to, you can really go to town on this demonstration: have them imagine their entire body is made of solid iron and their arm is completely locked in place. Give them a few moments to really feel that happening, then try to move their arm— the difference is incredible!

If you want to take this to the next level and have a little fun, you can transform your rigid arm demonstration into a simple hypnotic suggestibility trick. Once you've tried to push their arm out of position and failed and you've instructed them to imagine that their arm is totally locked in place, get them to repeat 'My arm is locked in place, my arm is locked in place' over and over as you say (and use these exact words!!) 'Continue to affirm that your arm is locked in place over and over, and as you do, I want you to try in vain to move your arm that is totally locked in place now.'

Most people will be unable to move their arm at all! To return everything back to normal, just say, 'When I click my fingers, everything will be back as it should be', then click your fingers and tell them to stop everything and put their arm back down. What you've just witnessed (well what you would have witnessed if you had stopped reading and done the exercise... don't worry, I wouldn't have done it either! But do make an effort to do it later. It is worth it!) is how incredibly powerful affirmations are! Even if you only say them for a few moments and you don't really believe them! A simple affirmation like 'I am really weak' can instantly hinder your physical ability, just as stating that you're strong can substantially boost it. Think about the consequences from a lifetime of telling yourself that you're not worthy, too ugly, inherently stupid, or destined to fail at whatever you try! Scary, isn't it! A huge proportion of the population are doing this constantly.

Now think about what you might be able to accomplish if you constantly gave yourself positive empowering affirmations, such as 'I'm really healthy', 'I feel fantastic', 'I'm always happy', or even 'Everyday, I have amazing life changing ideas worth billions!' Most people aren't disciplined enough to continually praise themselves, but that's OK. You can simply get the affirmation software to do that for you! By using affirmation software, every moment you spend at your computer can be utilised to help you achieve your desires. This is fantastic news as it means you're able to 'work' on your self development as you 'play', which removes a lot of guilt!

I'm using one of these programs right now, and as I type these words, I'm absorbing powerful affirmations that I specifically designed to help my writing flow more easily and avoid writer's block! I have several different affirmation lists that I run depending on what I'm doing on my computer. That's one of the real beauties of the software; you can just set it to program your mind to achieve whatever you desire and then forget all about it. (For more information see www.affirmagen.com)

Affirmations aside for a sec, there is a great NLP technique that I often use in circumstances when I feel I need that little bit extra; it's called the swish pattern. If you've used the swish before and not had much success, bear with me because this is my Turbo-Swish version! I call it the 'Swish Catapult'; you'll see why in a moment. To do the swish, you need to create two mental images. The first image we'll call image number one. This is your situation as it is now, so it shows the thing (or belief) that you want to change. Don't spend too long creating this image, keep it black and white and two dimensional, like a photograph.

The second imagine (image number two) is a representation of what you want. This could be absolutely anything. It might be a briefcase full of money, a shiny sports car, a sexy new body, or a big castle in the country. Whatever you picture, make sure that you pull out all the stops, and make the image so appealing and exciting that you practically drool just thinking about it. If you're doing this to change your beliefs, see yourself as you'd appear after you've adopted that new belief. You might hear yourself confidently stating the new belief or watch yourself doing something incredible now that you've accepted it and believe that it's possible. This second image should be 3D, and it should be moving too, so this time it's more like a huge 3D movie that you can step right inside. You also want to see yourself in the image. So if your image is of stacks of cash, see yourself throwing bills in the air and rolling around in it! If it's a swanky new sports car, see yourself in the driver's seat with a huge cheesy grin on your face!

Next, it's time to really crank it up. Introduce some booming music, fanfare trumpets, cheering crowds, wolf whistling fans, and rapturous applause. Now turn on the smells! Anything that's appropriate and appealing, throw it right in… a new car smell, soft leather, crispy new bank notes, your favourite perfume! Whatever's appropriate for your creation, throw it right in there.

As you fill your creation with a host of wonderful textures, feelings, sights, sounds, tastes, and smells, I want you to become aware of a huge dial that you can use to crank everything right up! As you turn the dial, it cranks up your anticipation, your excitement, and desire. Your creation grows bigger and bigger, it moves even closer and surrounds you completely—the colours grow brighter, the sounds more exciting, and everything glows with total joy! This is image number two.

OK… now, grab image number two and imagine you are cramming the entire thing into the pocket of an enormous slingshot. (That's the part which usually holds the stone!) On either side of the pocket are huge lengths of elastic that connect to either side of your head. As you cram your mouth watering creation inside, a force pulls the pocket away from you, and you hear the elastic creaking under the strain. When the elastic is at full stretch, bring back image number one. Look at this image as it represents your current situation. Hold it up in front of you, but imagine that it is actually printed on a piece of sugar glass (fake glass used for stunts in films). As you look at this image, become aware that you can see through the faded print and can just make out the catapult in the distance.

Count down from 3… 2… 1! Now, unleash the catapult, and imagine wind rushing past your face as your creation speeds towards you. As it smashes though the sugar glass your old way of thinking shatters into billions of pieces and is blasted behind you. At that very moment, you are totally absorbed in the new creation. As you do this, be sure that you actually enter the representation of you that was in the image you created and absorb all of the qualities they have.

Once you're completely inside, grab that dial again and crank everything up higher and higher!! Hear all of the sounds, feel the sensations, smell the glorious odours, become totally associated with the experience, and above all... enjoy every bit of it! You can use this technique as often as you desire to elicit all kinds of change; its great fun to do and incredibly powerful! The most important thing to remember is to have fun! It's your imagination, and no one can pry on your private thoughts, so spice it up as much as you dare, and make it as appealing as you possibly can. The more fun you have, the more effective it'll be.

We've talked a lot about how your beliefs condition your reality and the way you automatically attract the object of your focus with the assistance of emotions. We're now going to look at a state that really brings all that together, which is the state of expectation. When you expect to receive something, your ability to manifest it in your life is considerably magnified. Expect it, and it will be yours. You already know how to manifest anything you desire. You understand and appreciate that your beliefs, focus, and emotions create your reality. However, when you set forth a creation in this reality, a time lag exists before you receive it, and it's this lag that has blinkered us from our role in the creative process. This time lag protects us from the realisation of 'every single thought' and ensures that we receive only that which we commit to through the power of attention and dedication.

In the beginning, it often requires considerable persistence to turn a thought into reality; however, when you introduce expectation, all that changes. When you set forth a creative thought with the power of emotion and truly expect it to manifest in your reality, it will. A sense of expectation is one of the most powerful ways of boosting the power of your cosmic orders. When you truly expect results, they appear much more quickly. Next, we are going to explore the actual placing of the order itself. The way you deliver your request to the cosmos will affect the results you receive. To ensure that the cosmos hears you loud and clear, you need to focus on...

Boosting the Signal

✝ enter into a Natural Hypnotic trance & read your affirmations

One of the most commonly accepted ideas about creating your own reality is that of cosmic ordering. It's as though you were literally calling up a cosmic warehouse and actually placing an order for whatever it is you desire. I love this approach. It's very easy to do and makes a lot of sense. It's also similar to the more conventional way we gain things here in the physical world, so it's easy to relate to with very little or no practise.

Part of this cosmic ordering process is to somehow communicate your desire to the cosmos so that it knows what you want delivered. The variables that we have already discussed go a long way to improving that communication and making sure you ask for precisely what it is you desire. We are now going to consider a very simple technique that substantially boosts every cosmic order that you make. If you imagine that your cosmic orders are actually phone calls you make on your mobile phone, then these techniques will ensure that you have a full signal so that the cosmos can hear your order loud and clear!

By altering the frequency of your brainwaves, you are able to substantially boost this signal. In order to do this, simply allow yourself to enter an altered state of consciousness—in other words... RELAX! The most effective ways of doing this would be to use meditation or self hypnosis, but not many people have such a tool at their disposal, so we're going to cut a few corners to speed things up a little. As you progress with your manifestations, I strongly urge you to develop your meditative abilities and practise self hypnosis at least twice daily. Adding a few minutes of quiet focused meditation to your daily routine in the morning as you wake and again in the evening as you retire to bed will have a massive impact on your ability to consciously create your chosen reality.

Hypnosis isn't the mystical phenomenon that most people believe it to be. It's just a state of consciousness that differs slightly from the one that you usually use. The so called hypnotic state isn't as elusive as most people expect, and you certainly don't need to go through an induction to achieve it. Trance states happen all of the time, but we barely even notice them. Throughout the course of a normal day, we often drift in and out of varying states of consciousness all by ourselves.

Some of these states happen totally naturally as we move through our natural cycles of rest and active awareness; others are triggered by something outside of ourselves. It's these triggers that we are going to take advantage of to bypass the induction process and enable you to substantially boost your cosmic creation process without having to learn self hypnosis the normal way. This fast track approach has many advantages over the conventional process. Natural trance states are usually much more relaxing than their induced counterparts. They also allow you to experience deep trance states without having to learn how to achieve them. As we already know, the process of getting there is the emotion of being there, so once you've experienced the emotions of deep trance, to recall them using your internal senses is usually more than enough to get them back in the future. So essentially, what you're actually doing here is learning self hypnosis... backwards!

126

Natural trance triggers (things that cause you to go into a trance) are numerous. Some you'll discover are unique to yourself, such as a smell or a song that has special meaning to you. Others are more universal, like gazing into the flames of a fire or focusing on the pinpoint reflections of a highly polished surface. Simply sitting quietly and petting an animal is often enough to elicit a sufficient change in consciousness to substantially increase the power of your connection to the cosmos. Perhaps, one of the most common trance triggers is driving. If you have ever suddenly realised you can't remember the last couple of miles of your journey, then you've just come out of a natural trance state. Cars are particularly hypnotic for several reasons—they are warm and comfortable, they allow you to play relaxing music, and if it's raining, your windscreen wipers create a very hypnotic rhythmic beat. If you're particularly bored or tired, which is common on long journeys, you'll be close to trance anyway, and the additional focus of attention on the end of the road completes an assortment of hypnotic ingredients that any professional hypnotist would strive to include in a more conventionally prepared induction.

Going into trance while driving sounds incredibly scary, but you have nothing to worry about. Your subconscious mind simply takes over the process and is probably a much better driver than you are anyway; falling asleep while driving is something to worry about! Hypnotic audio programs can cause you to fall asleep as they are designed to relax you into trance, so never ever use any hypnotic audio in a vehicle. Whether you are using a prepared hypnotic induction or entering a trance state naturally, there are some specific things that cause hypnosis. The most effective of these are fixation of attention, relaxation, and a rhythmic movement or sound. When you are able to find something that naturally produces these effects, it is usually very hypnotic. The rhythmic sound of the ocean lapping against the shore is particularly effective, as it creates an association with relaxation because we are usually relaxing on holiday when we hear this sound.

You'll often find trance triggers in the most unexpected of places. When I worked at Dominos Pizza, I was regularly hynotized by the pizza oven! The oven had a rotating belt made from wire mesh that you could see through to the floor. As you looked down through the belt waiting for the pizza to make its way through the oven, you would see the belt moving in two directions at once as it looped back under itself. This created a rippling effect similar to a moiré pattern that was incredibly mesmerising, and even though I usually find conventional hypnosis difficult to follow, I could look at this for only a few seconds before I'd be in a deep trance.

Narrowing down your focus of attention has long been accepted as a trigger for hypnosis. By using something shiny, you are able to fixate your attention on a single point, which is a very effective way of achieving the trance state. This process was discovered purely by accident when the Scottish ophthalmic surgeon, James Braid, noticed that a patient in his waiting room had become fixated on the pin-point reflections of a highly polished old brass lamp. Braid recognised signs of trance in the patient and performed some preliminary tests to confirm his suspicions. Following his discovery, fixation of attention quickly became the standard induction process of many hypnotists, and the swinging pocket watch induction was born. A narrowing of attention doesn't have to be on a visual thing. It can be on a concept or idea. You'll often drift into trance while reading as you become increasingly engaged in the story.

Gazing into a candle flame, or better still, the flames of an open fire is incredibly hypnotic and a fantastic way to access deep trance states without needing a conventional induction. If you combine this with relaxing music, some simple deep breathing exercises, and perhaps a relaxing scent, you'll have a very hypnotic experience that will feel much more natural and relaxing than using a self hypnotic induction if you are not familiar with the techniques yet. To assist your relaxation, you can use some very simple techniques to boost the process. Simply closing your eyes and focusing on your breathing is enough to elicit a trance like state. If you want to deepen the state, then slowly count each in-breath and softly say the word 'Relax' every time you exhale. Keep your attention on your breathing, and if you notice that a thought has distracted you, imagine it floating away and bring your attention back to counting again.

One of the easiest ways to begin using altered states is to allow yourself to enjoy the natural ones that are already part of your everyday experience. Most people are often 'too busy' to allow themselves to relax and snap themselves back to full waking consciousness the moment they notice any shift in their attention. Whenever you catch yourself daydreaming or gazing off into deep nothingness, just let go and enjoy it. If you're at work, take a quick toilet break! Using these natural cycles is incredibly beneficial to your health. They also establish a deep connection with your higher self making any affirmations or cosmic orders during this time much more powerful. You'll often notice a sweet sensation in your muscles when you enter such a state. You'll feel calm, happy, relaxed, and at peace. View these special moments as gifts from your higher self and really enjoy them. The best way to use your affirmations when you notice yourself in such a state is to simply allow them to flow through you. The state will last just a few short minutes, but afterwards, you'll feel invigorated. You might even notice that the air around you feels cleaner, and you'll often enjoy a much greater clarity of vision, especially in the quality and vibrancy of colours. You might even like to create an anchor during these natural altered states so that you can access them more easily when it's convenient. If it helps, carry a note card at all times with your most important affirmations printed on it. Then whenever you shift into a natural altered state, you can read them quietly to yourself. Just read off one affirmation at a time, and really allow yourself to feel all of the associated emotions flood through your body before you move on to the next. Remember to create a sense of expectation as you deliver your suggestions to the cosmos knowing that the process itself is all that is required to cause your desire to begin to manifest in your life. Placing your order with the cosmos isn't the end of the process; you now need to prepare yourself to...

Receive Your Order

There are several things you need to do in order to ensure that you receive whatever it is you have ordered from the cosmos. However, the most important step isn't something that you should do, but something that you shouldn't. Many people try to get too involved in the process and end up stifling the ability of the cosmos to bring their desires or blinding themselves to whatever it is they have ordered when it does arrive. Detaching yourself from the process completely allows the cosmos to deliver your request in the very best and most appropriate way possible.

Your part in the cosmic ordering process is to simply ask for whatever it is you desire. Deciding how, when, and from where your desire will appear is the job of the cosmos itself. There will be practically unlimited ways that the cosmos will be able to bring whatever you have ordered into your life. If you enter into the process with preconceived ideas of how your requests will be met, you are closing off countless avenues of delivery. The object of your desire begins its journey into your reality the moment you place your very first order with the cosmos. Some people believe that subsequent orders for the same item will actually stop it from manifesting, as though each time you place an order the sending process is reset. This isn't true; you can continue to order something as many times as you desire, and the more attention and focus you give to that thing, the faster it will arrive in your reality. However, it is important that you understand that it is on its way to you from the very first order, and each order following that will bring it even closer, not reset the process.

In certain situations, there is benefit to be gained from placing a solitary request. When you place the initial order, your expectation will be high, and your emotions will be in alignment with your desire ensuring that the correct vibration is created to attract it into your life. If you then completely forget about the object you have ordered, you will not hinder its journey into your reality, but when you continue to focus on an object, you can become frustrated that it has not yet arrived. It is this frustration that prevents it from manifesting at all. At this point, your focus has shifted from having the thing that you desire to the lack of having it. You must, at all times, focus on what you desire. If you focus on the lack of what you desire, you will push what you desire away and attract an increasing lack of what you desire into your life. When you can focus on what you desire and you know that it is on its way to you, it will manifest in your reality. You can place just one cosmic order per desire if you wish. You will still create it in your life. But when you continue to focus on your desire over and over, you attract it into your life much quicker.

If you want something to manifest in your life and you order it in the correct way using the techniques you have learned throughout this book, that thing cannot fail to appear. From the very first moment you place an order with the cosmos, the cosmos begins the delivery process. Depending on what you have ordered, the way you placed the order, and your belief about having it, the time it takes to appear can vary dramatically. If you want to keep that time lag to a minimum and enjoy your cosmic creations as quickly as possible, it's important that you are open to receiving your order, remain unbiased with regard to its origin, and follow any inner guidance you receive about getting it. From the moment you place an order, your higher self will be directing you to its realisation. This subtle direction will often appear in your consciousness as an innocent thought that offers an alternative to your daily routine— you might decide to walk to work one day and leave the car at home and in the process bump into an old friend that is trying to get rid of the very thing you desire.

When you listen to your inner guidance, such synchronicities are commonplace and will considerably reduce the time required for your order to manifest in your reality. Of all the different techniques you can use to develop your ability to create the reality you desire, there is one process that takes your manifestation to a whole new level— the realisation of your life purpose. When you are working in alignment with a higher purpose, you're literally going with the flow. When you begin to work in this area, conscious effort isn't necessary to realise your dreams, as their actualisation is an unavoidable and natural progression of the path you are already on.

Aligning your physical goals and desires with your higher purpose is an incredible way of manifesting your true desire at a level that goes beyond the ego, allowing your experience to truly nourish your soul. Focusing on your higher purpose brings you a reality that is rich with love which affects all levels of existence, and the ripples of success are echoed here in the physical world, as well as the higher dimensions. This process creates tremendous abundance in all areas of your life; the ripples that reach down to the slower vibrations of the physical plane will verify your perception of success in the possessions you attract and the people you meet.

Working towards your life purpose is extremely rewarding and puts you firmly in the fast lane of manifestation. Information, people, physical items, and tools simply appear as you need them. You go through life effortlessly, and everything you desire is available to you in abundance exactly when you need it. Operating in this realm feels very much as though you were a conduit of energy, like a channel that is wide open allowing reality to flow through freely without any need or desire to hold on to anything. Things come easily, and it's just as easy to let them go; you have no need for anything, for everything is flowing through you in perfect order.

This is living in the flow; it's a place to which every one of us has access and entering it is as simple as recognising the reason you are here. The flow is waiting for you, eager to provide you with everything you need to actualise the dreams of your soul, and as you become aware of your life purpose, you elevate yourself above the congestion and feel its loving caress like a refreshing cool summer breeze. Operating within your life purpose and acting solely for the good of mankind isn't a requirement of manifestation. You can manifest anything you desire, and many things that you don't, very easily with disciplined focus. However, working against your higher purpose can feel like a struggle. Manifestation often requires a higher degree of conscious effort, things take longer to appear, and possessions can bring lessons that may be costlier than their worth.

Manifestation that supports your spiritual growth or contributes to the greater good of mankind is infinitely more powerful and rewarding than that created out of greed. That said, you should not stifle your growth or sacrifice your desires in order to feel more spiritual. Many people feel that financial abundance is in some way evil or perverse and one must be poor to be spiritual. This isn't true. It's simply an unfortunate program that most people have allowed to corrupt the fertile ground of their subconscious mind. Money is simply energy, and as you open the channels that allow it to flow freely through you, more will indeed come; you will be able to use this in any way you desire. To continue your life's work and serve the greater good of mankind better, you may need to step outside of the 'rat race' to allow time to focus on your own spiritual growth. This is a tremendously empowering thing to be able to do, and it certainly requires money to do it. Being poor, or living with only very basic possessions, reinforces a concept of lack. There is much more than enough for everyone to experience a truly abundant reality, and denying yourself your desires isn't a fast track ticket to a more spiritual life.

Working towards your higher purpose will take you in a very joyful and rewarding direction. Every decision or action you take that moves you further along your own spiritual path takes you higher into the flow; manifestation becomes easier and easier as you ascend beyond effort and open up to the possibilities that present themselves. Operating within the flow and making decisions or taking actions that move you into it will have a notably different effect on you than those decisions that are not in alignment with your higher purpose. By paying close attention to how you feel when you make life choices, you can begin to recognise your own higher purpose enabling you to begin living your life in true alignment with your soul's desires. Many of the decisions you make in life, especially those relating to your career, will change your progression along your spiritual path. Some will speed it up, others will slow it down, some may cause you to wander from your path or even go backwards, and some will feel as though you have stopped completely. Ideally, you should only make decisions and take actions that empower you and help you to progress as a spiritual being. Whenever you are faced with a decision ask yourself which choice offers you the most joy, for it is this choice that is in alignment with your higher purpose. If you are unable to discern which options bring you greater joy, ask which helps you to better serve humanity. Your higher purpose will always serve the greater good of mankind in some way. If you can recognise this quality in your options, then it is safe to assume that this route will bring you greater abundance.

Sometimes, when you are faced with a decision, walking the higher path might not appear to be the most logical solution to a problem, but it will always 'feel' like the 'right' decision. For many years, I have felt that my life purpose is to communicate spiritual wisdom to others and to help them to live more abundant lives. In order to do this, I've studied various areas very extensively, tested my discoveries, and then packaged them into texts such as this one. Before I began writing about cosmic ordering and manifestation, I was working with hypnosis and NLP and produced many 'how to' guides and videos to help others use the techniques I'd found so useful. Eventually, I launched a website to promote my books and videos, and this very quickly became my main source of income. I received very favourable feedback from my readers, and everything seemed to be going great. My online business has never earned me a fortune, but it provided me with enough to be able to focus on my own spiritual growth without having to work a regular job. Recently, as you know from the first chapter, I bought a new home. This turned out to be much more expensive than I expected; I had no idea how many fees were involved in moving as I'd only ever rented accommodation, so I was now faced with a rather sticky situation. My online business wasn't generating enough extra income to cope with the unforeseen expenses of the move, so something had to change. I either needed an unexpected windfall, or I needed to boost my sales. Logic was telling me to try to boost sales. I had a list of email addresses for everyone that had previously purchased my books and videos, and I knew they were interested in material on hypnosis and NLP, so I figured I could quickly produce something they'd find useful and mail out an advert to the list. This is what logic and reason were telling me to do, but it didn't feel like the right thing to do. Even though I knew my existing customers would go for it, I felt as though I would in some way be ripping them off. Trying to make a quick buck with a flash promotion of a thrown together product didn't feel as though I were acting with integrity, and it certainly didn't feel as though it were in alignment with my higher purpose, so I began to ask questions.

I asked myself what it was I really wanted to do if money was not a factor; I asked what would better serve the greater good of mankind; I asked what brought me the most joy and gave me a true feeling inside that I was doing something right, and I came to the conclusion that if I already had the extra cash I needed, I would simply give the information away. I wouldn't need to sell it. As soon as I'd made the decision to do this, I remembered that I'd already created three audio files that my customers would love. I'd recorded them a few months earlier hoping to include them in a future promotion, but I'd never got around to using them for anything. Making the decision to give those files away felt very empowering; it felt like the right thing to do and was in complete alignment with my higher purpose. That night I wrote an email that included the three audio files and sent it out to my list of customers. The email didn't offer anything for sale; it simply explained what I'd been up to recently and included the links needed to listen to the audio files. I sent the email and headed off to bed.

Logic would have put a price tag on the audio files and sent out a sales letter to the same list hoping to generate a few extra sales to help with the expense of the move. I didn't do that. Logic would have viewed my actions as a wasted opportunity. I didn't. To me it felt as though I'd done something right, something that had elevated me into the flow, and from here, I knew that whatever I needed would be provided in perfect time and perfect order. The following morning as I turned on my computer and waited for my email inbox to load, I already knew that giving the information away was the right thing to do. As the page loaded, I found a very pleasant surprise. Although I hadn't offered anything for sale in the mailing I'd sent out only a few hours ago, my sales were up... seriously up! By the end of the day, my daily sales figures were up by more than 300% over the daily average of the previous month's sales figures.

A sceptic would rightfully suggest that this sudden increase in sales was to be expected. I would be the first to agree that if you give something away, people often feel obligated to give you something back in return even if you don't ask for anything; that's just human nature. I'd expected a few extra sales from people making their way back to my website and buying something out of obligation or even appreciation of the free gift, but I hadn't expected such a huge increase from one mailing. When I logged into my sales statistics and began taking a closer look at the night's activities, I found that every sale I'd generated that day had been from a completely new customer! Now, this isn't so easily explained away by the hardened sceptic. This wasn't human nature at work; it was the spiritual laws of abundance and attraction. I'd given away a quality product to people that really appreciated it; in return, something I needed had been given to me. It was simply another example of how energy moves through the universe, especially when we do things that are in alignment with our higher purpose. Most people that have faith in something beyond science will agree that you reap what you sow. When you put something positive out to the world, the world will give you something positive in return. The spiritual laws of abundance and karma are not so constrained that your reward must come from those that benefit from your generosity. My karmic payment for the free audio files I'd emailed to my existing customers came from a new source, and because I was operating in alignment with my higher purpose, it came almost immediately.

I don't want you to fall into the trap of thinking that these techniques will only work if you're ordering something righteous or spiritual; you can create absolutely anything you desire. Creating your reality is something that is completely unavoidable. The universal laws that govern all of creation apply to you whether you understand them or not. When you understand how to create consciously, you can have whatever you desire. If you desire a bigger house, a fancy sports car, and a slimmer, sexier body, you can have them. It doesn't matter if having those things appears wrong or immoral. You can have anything you desire, so long as you ask for it in the correct way. You now know the secrets of creation; you know how to manifest into your life absolutely anything you desire; you have unlimited wishes at your disposal. The question you should be asking yourself now is…

What Do I Want To Create?

The question 'What do I want to create?' is often much more difficult to answer than one might expect. Most people haven't really given much thought to what they want in life aside of knowing its something different to what they already have but don't want! Usually, if you're suffering in a particular area, you tend to focus on the suffering. For most people, when someone asks you what you want, your immediate reaction is to tell them what you don't want. Most people can tell you what they don't want in such depth and with such precision that it's obvious they've spent a huge amount of time thinking about it, and if you push them to tell you what they do what, they often continue giving you a list of things they don't. Many people's version of a positive shift in focus is to stop saying 'I don't want to be fat' and start saying 'I want to stop being fat!!' That's not positive at all; it's totally focused on what you don't want! If you think that you want to stop being fat, what you really want is to be slim!

That's an enormous difference, and you need to completely grasp it before you begin creating your wish list. The direction of your focus is paramount to your success. You must focus on whatever it is you desire. Unfortunately, when you ask most people to list the reasons they want to make a desired change, you usually end up with a huge detailed list of negative things that they want to move away from or avoid and a tiny list of ambiguous positive things that they want to move toward, such as 'I want to be rich' or 'I want to be healthy'. The general opposite of what you don't want isn't usually a stimulating enough goal to elicit the emotional shift required to create it.

If you want to be rich, then you should make a very specific list of the things you want to own, the amount of money you want to earn (or win!), the vehicle you want to drive (or fly), and the place you want to live etc. etc. The more specific and detailed you can be the better! Remember, placing an order with the cosmos is like calling someone up on your phone; if you want to talk to a specific person, you must dial a specific number. So if you want to create a specific thing, you must place an order for that specific thing. What you choose to create is up to you. It's usually easier to start by creating things that are similar to those which you already own and that you believe you can have. This is because the vibration at which those items resonate is very similar to the vibration you are currently sending out into the cosmos. In order to attract something into your life, you must first align yourself with it. By following the advice given in the previous chapters, you can, with practice, align yourself to any reality you desire.

do this

The big mistake that most people make when they begin to use these techniques is to create things that they believe will satisfy a need, only to find that, later when that thing has appeared in their life, it does not, and they have to start the process all over again. Choose something that you want to create right now, and ask yourself why you want it. List all of the things that you think you will have or gain when you have created this thing in your life. Many people create material objects because they believe they will satisfy emotional needs. It's very important to uncover the emotional need behind each item you are going to create as it is always much more effective to simply attract that emotion into your being, rather than a thing that you believe will bring it to you. To do this, always ask yourself why you want it. Keep on asking this question over and over until you find the root need that has lead to your desire. Then magnetise that into your reality. If you want a new career because you think it will make you feel more secure, then magnetise the sensation of security first. Allow this to manifest in whatever way the cosmos decides is best for you, and then order the new career if you still feel you want it. Focusing on creating the qualities of the object you desire is much more powerful than focusing on the actual object alone.

What you now choose to create is in your hands. Standing here, ready to take the first steps into your new reality might leave you wondering what you might like to create first. The best way to use these techniques is to enjoy them, play with the different ideas presented throughout the book, and find out which suit you best. It helps to start on things that you don't really need—parking spaces are a great example, as well as material items very similar to those that you already own.

start small to build your ability

Many people fall into the trap of only using cosmic ordering on things they really need or find difficult to obtain using more conventional techniques. Unfortunately, this can often lead to failure and result in an increasing lack of faith in the process itself. This is because of the difficulty that people have letting go. If you are desperate for something, then your focus is often on wanting that thing so much that you push it away. Leave the big stuff for the time being, and come back to it when you've developed more confidence in your ability to create things. You should aim to use the techniques as often as possible; every action that you take will harvest more favourable results if you work with the subtle energies first.

As you use the techniques more regularly, you become a much more powerful creator. Conditioning yourself through regular practise will require some effort and discipline during the first few weeks, but you will quickly find that you are using energy work in every decision you make and your creations will be much more rewarding as a result.

I want to personally thank you for allowing me to share this information with you. I've been using these techniques for a few years now, and they've had a tremendous impact on every area of my life. People are attracted to cosmic ordering for all kinds of reasons—for some, it simply comes down to a desire for more; for others, it is something much more spiritual.

For me, cosmic ordering is much more than creating a comfortable life; it's a powerful connection to the higher-self that enables an individual to grow as a spiritual being. I personally believe that we will very soon transcend as a race into a fourth dimensional reality. When this happens, the lag that currently protects us from our negative creations will be removed, and it is learning to control our creations now, while we still have a buffer in place, that will enable us to make the shift into the next dimension as smooth as possible. If you would like to find out more about these ideas, I strongly recommend reading 'The Ancient Secrets of the Flower of Life' by Drunvalo Melchizedek. Of course, a belief in dimensional shifts and spiritual evolution on a global scale isn't necessary to benefit from using these techniques. You can use these techniques to attract anything into your life, so play with them, enjoy them, and allow yourself to have the life you've always desired.

You deserve it!

Remember...

"The process of getting whatever you desire is the emotion of already having it!"

...Now Take Action!

If you are interested in the possibility of earning a residual income by helping me spread this knowledge, please visit my website for information on affiliate opportunities at:

www.cosmicorderingsecrets.com/affiliate.htm

For more information on cosmic ordering and to discover new and exciting ways to improve your life effortlessly please go to:

www.cosmicorderingsecrets.com/info.htm

To view my personal top 10 recommended books list and find out which books have changed my life visit:

www.cosmicorderingsecrets.com/top10.htm

To find out more about automated affirmation software please visit www.affirmagen.com

I encourage you to take action and prove to yourself that cosmic ordering really does work. Once you have, please pass this book on to a friend and allow it to change their life too!

Made in the USA
Coppell, TX
20 September 2020

38448667R00090